1

To all survivors of abuse everywhere, and for those still in it, you are braver than you know.

Warning - before we start it is fair to say that the topics covered in this book are not pleasant and may be very difficult to read about for people who have suffered or are still suffering at the hands of an abuser/narcissist. Proceed with caution and take your time.

I'd also like to say that I am not a trained psychologist, I am just someone who has been unfortunate enough to have massive amounts of experience of being abused by a narcissist. Everything in this book comes either from my own personal experiences, or from the experiences of other survivors/victims that have spoken to me and want their stories to be shared.

Please could you take the time to leave a review on Amazon, as this helps other people who need a resource like this to find the book by making it more visible. My goal is to create awareness for these serious issues, and you review helps to do that.

Thank you so much.

Introduction

What can men do against such reckless hate?

Theoden - The Lord of the Rings: The Two Towers

Anyone who knows me can tell you that I love The Lord of the Rings. I love the escapism, the fantasy, the grandeur, but I also love the messages of hope amidst hardship.

This book will be about that. It will shine a spotlight on the hardships, but also show the hope. Every story in this book comes from a male victim of domestic abuse, and while terrible in nature, every single one of them is now free of the abuse and moving on with life.

First off, let's take a look at how this book will work in terms of layout and flow. Each chapter will be a new story. As mentioned above, each story is from an actual survivor of domestic abuse. Each chapter will tell their story of an incident of abuse, and then we will unpack it. I'll highlight what types of abuse were involved, what tools their abuser used against them, my thoughts on why, and if possible, any potential tips or advice for anyone who suffers a similar incident of abuse.

This book won't give detailed descriptions and definitions of the types of abuse there are, or the types of tools abusers/narcissists use on their victims. I have covered all of those in my previous book "Why didn't you just leave them? And other ignorant things people say about abusive relationships". I'd recommend reading that book first if you want to have a solid foundation and understanding around these topics before diving into actual survivor stories.

Each story will be told in the first person, as it has been told to me. I'll also say up front that I will tell them truthfully, so if the language was bad that was used against them, I will use it as told. So, expect bad language, and horrible things that are said.

No names will be given, as while the owners of these stories want them to be shared, they want them done so anonymously. I will say though that these stories come from people around the world. I am based in the United Kingdom, but these stories span across multiples countries and continents.

As I said above, we won't go into details around the tools and techniques of abusers, but throughout the ten stories that follow we will cover various forms of abuse, and various different abusive tools.

To name a few upfront, so that you know what to expect, we will cover:

- Emotional Abuse
- Physical Abuse
- Verbal Abuse
- Mental Abuse
- Manipulation
- Lies
- Gaslighting
- Isolation
- Blame Shifting
- Pre-Empting
- Fear and threats
- And many more tools and techniques of the abuser/narcissist.

Even though this book is written by a man, and the stories are all of men who have been abused at the hands of women, I truly believe that this book can benefit anyone who reads it. Many of the same principles apply in all abusive relationships, whether it's a male or female victim, and the knowledge gained by reading books such as these is invaluable to bring this terrible topic into the light it so very much deserves.

It's only by talking about these topics, and educating everyone about them, that we can start to make the changes that are needed in society, and in the legal processes and procedures currently in place, and try to combat this epidemic that threatens men, women, children, and any one of any race, gender, belief, religion, size, shape, sexual orientation, and more.

As I emphasized in my previous book, abuse is about control. Knowledge is the first tool that we as victims and survivors can use to combat the tools of the abusers and narcissists.

So, whether you are a victim, survivor, or someone wanting to learn, let that be the purpose of this book. Knowledge. Take what you learn and share it with others. Encourage them to learn about these things too.

With that being said, let's dive into the stories. Let's learn, let's digest, and let's be a part of the tide that ensures that stories like this are not the stories of the future.

Chapter 1: An Abusive Rip Off

The first story comes from a man who was in a long-term relationship with his partner. They weren't married, as it seems she wanted to keep her options open, but they had been together for a few years, and for him, the "abuse" had started about a year previous. I say "abuse" because he didn't realise that it had started much earlier than that, but it was only when it became physical that he thought of it as abuse. This is something that I hope these books can help to combat – the belief that abuse is physical only. It is way more than that. Some people never get physically abused but are still in an abusive relationship.

As a recap from the introduction, each story will be told in the first person, and I am writing it as it was told to me, obviously keeping the story as it was told, but using my words to focus it. Anyone who has one of these stories to tell, can understand that when you tell it, it can wander, it can break, it can be tough, so I have tried to retell it without the wandering or breaks.

One interesting thing about this story, and actually the other nine that follow, is that in every single one, the male victim was physically bigger and stronger than their female abuser. Remember, abuse is not about size or strength, it's about control.

Based on that statement above, what I will do for some of the stories where I have been given permission by the teller, is give a few facts (height and weight) about the victim, to show exactly what I mean when I say that abuse it not about size.

The Story

Height: 6 foot 4 inches

Weight: 110kg/242lbs

It's funny because I don't remember anything else about that day except for what happened. I can't remember if it was summer, winter, hot, cold, nothing. I don't know what happened before it, or what happened after, I just remember "it". Even though it was probably 10 years ago I still remember it clear as anything.

She was yelling at me, again, and for what I couldn't tell you as it was such a frequent thing. I just remember being told off and sworn at and trying to keep myself busy in the house. I wasn't at work that day so it must have either been a weekend or I was on leave or something.

I went into the spare room, which also was the study, which was down the hall, away from the kitchen and lounge area where she was. I could still hear her swearing, muttering things about me, occasionally yelling to make sure I heard the insults, but I just carried on with what I was doing. It was nothing I hadn't heard before a million times anyway, just the generic "fucking useless, fucking pathetic, loser" and all of that.

I must have been trying to sort something on the desk, because I was standing not sitting, and she just kept going. Eventually it just got too much, and I couldn't ignore it anymore, so I said something back. I can't remember what, but whatever it was, she did not like it one bit. She never stopped the yelling, but I heard it getting closer and closer until she was through the door and in the room. She had a look on her face that was pure rage, and the best way I can put it, pure violence. I could see she wanted to hurt me.

She was screaming now, every single rude word she knew, and the angry demands "What the fuck did you just say to me? What did you say, you piece of shit? Big man speaking up, tell me now!".

I backed off a bit, to the edge of the desk, but it was up against the wall, so there was nowhere else for me to go, and she was between me and the doorway.

She was absolutely fuming, but I was scared to have yet another big blow-up fight, so I turned my head back to the desk and carried on with what I was doing, and I didn't say a word.

We had this thing on the left side of the desk, it was like a big stationery organiser - it had pens, little bits of paper, stapler, scissors, ruler etc. It was probably about 40cm long and weighted about 5 pounds at a guess. Well, next thing I knew that was being smacked around the left side of my face. It hurt obviously, but it was more the shock that got me. I remember stumbling back towards the window, trying to stop myself going through it.

She was not done, and clearly wanted more. She grabbed my hair and started pulling it hard, screaming in my face "What the fuck did you say to me?!". I could feel spit hitting the side of my face because she was so close, and the scream was so loud it was hurting my ear.

The weird thing is, I remember we weren't alone in the house. The cleaner was there that day, and I remember thinking that she must be hearing all of this, and surely, she was going to come in and see what was going on. She didn't, maybe she was outside or something, or just too scared.

All of this wasn't new. The screaming, the swearing, the hitting, the hair pulling. But then she did do something new. She let go of my hair and grabbed the neckline at the front side of my t-shirt that I was wearing, and she started to yank with all of her weight and force. I could feel the back of my neck getting rubbed raw, and I was getting pulled forward and down. She was going absolutely crazy. "I bought you this, give it to me!!". I still remember thinking "What the fuck? This is ridiculous."

The t-shirt started to rip, and it started splitting in two, from the neckline down. It was probably split to just down below my chest when she let go for one second. I ran. I ran out of the room, and into the hallway, heading towards the kitchen where I thought the cleaner might be. I remember just shouting for the cleaner, asking her to help. Asking her to get it to stop. The cleaner did hear me and came into the kitchen, just as my raging abuser caught up.

I still clearly remember thinking "Ok someone is here now; she won't keep going." But she did. I think she was so enraged, so lost in her anger and violence that she wasn't thinking about anything else. She grabbed my t-shirt and started pulling again. I was yelling for the cleaner to get her to stop, and the cleaner was saying over and over "Stop it, stop it".

My t-shirt ripped in half, all the way from the neckline to the bottom at the front, and she grabbed it at the back and pulled it off me. Despite everything going on, I remember being so embarrassed. I was standing shirtless in front of the cleaner, I had scratches from fingernails down my front, the left side of my face was all red from being hit, and my neck had a raw red line across the back of it from the t-shirt. I felt so pathetic and so small.

I just stood there, the cleaner just stood there (she clearly had no idea what to do or say anymore, and I don't blame her), and now that she had the t-shirt off of me, my abuser started to obviously realise that she had been seen doing what she just did. I could see she was calculating what next. For a second, I hoped that now that it had been witnessed, it would be over. It wasn't then and wasn't for a long time after that. She said something along the lines of "He's going to try and lie about what happened, he's a liar, it was him".

She grabbed her car keys off the counter, took the t-shirt and ran outside to the car and drove off. I stood there for a second more, then went straight to the bedroom to get a new shirt on to try and hide my embarrassment.

I found the cleaner still in the kitchen, and tried to talk to her, but it was hard to get words out properly. I felt so ashamed. It was bad enough what happened, but the fact that someone had seen it made it worse for some reason. I remember I apologised to the cleaner for what had happened, paid her, and said she could go home. She never came back again.

I literally have no idea what I did next, or what happened after that on that day, but I did later find out that she had taken the t-shirt to a public bin a few blocks away and thrown it away so that I couldn't take pictures of it or show it to anyone, and had driven straight to see her family to tell them her version of the story, which didn't resemble reality in any way at all. I was the abuser, and her the victim in everything that happened, and there was no evidence to say otherwise. When I ever tried to discuss it with her after that day, the story she gave me changed as well. It was one of how she tried to talk to me calmly because I was being rude, and that I hit her, and she was just defending herself. Typical.

The Unpacking

Physical abuse, check. Verbal abuse, check. But what else? It's easy and obvious to see those and not really worry about anything else, but this is why narcissists and abusers are so good at what they do, because they layer on different types of abuse and different tools and techniques, that you don't see them all unless you know.

Let's start with the different types of abuse here, and then move on to the tools and techniques they used.

So, we have physical and verbal abuse, but what about emotional abuse? Breaking someone down, calling them things to lower their self-esteem, like loser, pathetic, useless, big man. That is definitely emotional abuse, as even though they are verbally delivering the abuse, the words are aimed at your self-worth, your core being. A person with low self-worth and low self-esteem is much easier to control. And let's not forget the humiliation here, of doing it in front of someone, taking their clothes off them and leaving them standing there embarrassed. An emotional blow for sure.

What about mental abuse? Knowing that if you open your mouth it could lead to this kind of attack? Knowing that if you get something from them, they can quite literally physically take it back, even if it means ripping it off your body? The mental repercussions of this incident were big for the victim and lasted well beyond that day.

Now let's look at some of the tools and techniques the abuser used here.

Fear – by physically attacking someone, hitting them, assaulting them, you create fear. He said he didn't want another big blow up so kept quiet, so he was afraid of that happening. It did anyway, and he was more scared after that day.

Criticism – all of the things that she said to him, all of the names she called him.

"It was nothing I hadn't heard before a million times anyway, just the generic "fucking useless, fucking pathetic, loser" and all of that."

It obviously was an ongoing thing from the way he told it, and again designed to crush his spirit, make him value himself less, and ultimately be easier to dominate.

Blame shifting – telling the cleaner that it was him and not her, that he is going to lie about it, when she literally had just done it in front of them. Telling him afterwards that it was his fault. All classic blame shifting to avoid any accountability. A narcissist can never be wrong. Ever.

Pre-empting – running to her family immediately and giving them her version of the story before he could. Classic behaviour of a narcissist, pre-empting everything they do, so that if the victim does it or says anything afterwards, they look like a liar.

My opinion, thoughts, advice, or tips

My opinion and thoughts on this are that it is just classic narcissist behaviour. Abuse, abuse, abuse, then blame shift and pre-empt. Not their fault, they did nothing wrong, you are the problem. It's something that will repeat itself as we go through the other stories. The blame can never fall at an abuser's or narcissist's feet, it must be you, not them.

When I was talking to the person whose story this is, he asked me what he could have done differently, what could have helped, made it easier, got him free. Honestly, this is such a difficult scenario to give advice on, as there isn't much subtle going on here, it is full blown and in your face, and he had to react to a violent and terrible situation.

I told him something that is going to sound very controversial, but once I explained it fully to him and why I was saying it, he understood as well.

The only thing that he could have done differently, and I am not saying that I would have done this, is to try to de-escalate it before it began. He could have apologised for saying something and tried to calm his abuser down. I know that sounds truly horrible, and it just seems so wrong, but this is not a perfect world, and in an abusive relationship, sometimes you just need to survive.

We discussed this a bit, and he thinks that it wouldn't have made a difference in that situation, as he felt she was too enraged to calm down. Either way, it's the only possible thing I could think of as additional advice for in the moment.

He didn't go to the police, and to be honest, I think if he had gone to them, and even if he had given them the cleaner's details as a witness, I don't think it would have made much difference. He was hurt yes – scratches, a bruised face, and a raw neck, but I don't think the police would have taken it seriously enough, as usually they don't understand the depths of narcissism either. He didn't have the shirt either as evidence. So, taking that scenario in isolation, I don't think there is much more he could have done during the incident.

One piece of advice I said to him that I always give people now, is to log it. Write it down while it is still fresh in your mind. Write down the date it happened, the time it happened, and as much detail as you can. Any pictures to accompany it would be great, like of the scratches, bruises etc. All of that evidence can come in handy one day, when you are trying to get out, or once you are out and in court or in a police investigation, for example. Obviously make sure that this logbook and evidence can't be found by your abuser. Hide it, keep it at work, in a lockbox somewhere, with a trusted friend, but make sure it doesn't get found, otherwise it will be destroyed, and you will pay a price from your abuser for having it.

Chapter 2: Tinder Tantrum

This story comes from a man who was married to his abuser. They had been married for a few years, and actually had a child together. They argued a lot, and she used various abusive tools and techniques against him, but no physical abuse had yet started. This story doesn't include any either. Not all abuse is physical, and not every scenario ends in violence, but every scenario does end in damage for the victim.

I'll tell the story and the extra bits as I got them.

The Story

This is something that has had quite a long-lasting impact on me. I really get worried it's going to happen again, and that no one will ever think I am enough for them.

This happened after we were married, we had been married about two or so years, and together for four, and we had a child together, they must have been about 9 or 10 months old at the time. At that point, I didn't understand that I was in an abusive relationship. She would be rude to me, put me down, say horrible things to me, scream, swear, demand things, but I didn't see it as abuse, I just saw it as not nice. It was only later when the physical stuff started that I thought I was being abused, and then way later when I was free from her that I realised I had been abused long before she hit me.

Anyway, one day I was sitting at home alone, and I was bored and just messing around on my phone. I had an Apple i-Phone, which is relevant as you'll see. I was just messing around with the settings, and trying to see if there were any more specific Apple only settings, as it was my first i-Phone. The only thing I had really setup was our Apple family account, which both my wife and I were on, as she also had an i-Phone. I went onto the settings for the family account, and was scrolling through them, when I noticed one that was about the apps that had been downloaded and installed. When I went on it, I wasn't expecting what I found. Under her name, it showed all of her downloads, and there, from about a month or so prior, was Tinder. Why the hell had she downloaded a dating app, never mind one that is widely regarded as just a hook up app?

I didn't know what to do, so I thought I would try and check her phone when she was asleep or showering or something. Maybe it was a mistake or something, I had no idea.

Later that night when baby was asleep, she went to have a bath, and left her phone charging in the kitchen. I felt dirty doing it, but I logged onto her phone as I knew the pin and started to have a look for Tinder. I found it and found all of the chats she had been having with guys since she had been on it. They were all super flirtatious, and while not explicit, some of them were fairly sexual.

I'm very anti-cheating, and believe that if you aren't happy, and want to move on, or find someone else, then you should tell the other person and break up, not go behind their back.

I went and confronted her straight away. Why do you have Tinder on your phone? Why are you talking to other men?

This was a big thing to me, and I think it would be to most people, so I was really shocked by the response I got. It wasn't apologetic, it wasn't embarrassed, it wasn't shame at being caught. It was disgusting. She went on a full-blown attack right out of the gate.

"Why are you on my phone? I'll talk to whoever I want. You can't tell me who I'm allowed to talk to!"

I couldn't believe the audacity, to basically cheat and then to turn it around, like I was the one who was in the wrong. I told her she is flirting and sending sexual messages to other men, and she is married, and has a baby with me. Again, I didn't get the kind of response I would have expected.

"First off, I'll talk to whoever the fuck I want, about anything I fucking want. And secondly if I want to go and fuck every guy on there I will. You work with women every day. Maybe I should go and fuck those guys, teach you a lesson."

This woman was seriously comparing me working in an office that had female staff, to being on Tinder and messaging other guys. What did she expect? That I could only work at all male jobs? I had never cheated, never flirted, nothing, and she knew I was very severely anti-cheating, having previously been cheated on by an ex years before, which obviously I had confided in her about. That's pretty important to know, because of what she came out with next.

"Your ex cheated on you, and I am talking to other guys, so clearly it's you that's the fucking problem if everyone you are with does it to you."

I didn't know what to say to that, or what to do, so I left. I grabbed a bag, threw a change of clothes in, and drove to a local hotel and stayed there for the night. She didn't try to contact me at all.

The next day at work, I chatted to one of my male colleagues about it. He agreed that it was ridiculous and that she was completely out of order for being on a dating site at all, never mind what she chatting about to other men.

I went home and tried to talk to her again, and again, and not for the last time, I was completely blindsided by what I got. In all of the shock at finding everything the night before, I didn't even think to take photos of the messages or anything like that. So, I had no proof, and she came with:

"I don't know what you are talking about. I downloaded Tinder to see what it was as I didn't know, and everyone always goes on about it. I don't even have an account, I havent been messaging anyone. Look."

She had deleted everything and was going with a full blanket denial. I told her I had seen them, read them, and she had reacted very differently the night before, and said disgusting things. I got another great one:

"What are you talking about? That never happened. I went to bath and when I came back you were gone. I tried to call you so many times, but it just went straight to voicemail."

Even then I knew it was complete bullshit, but I didn't know what to do or say. The sad thing is, I started to believe her story, because she stuck with it. Years later, I ended up finding way more apps on her phone, with the same kind of messages and even messages to her ex where she was trying to rekindle things with him. This was the guy she told me had cheated on her. Luckily, he was having none of it. Seems to me now that she must have cheated on him.

From being cheated on by an ex-girlfriend, and then a wife, I really started to think something was wrong with me. Why wasn't I enough? Could I ever trust anyone?

When I confronted her for those other apps, I got the same full-on assault as I did the first time. And I never got the complete denial after that, just more of the full-on vileness and disgusting things being said.

The Unpacking

Wow. That my response when he told me this story. Just wow. I have experienced similar and heard and seen a lot, but still when I hear someone else's stories of abuse it just makes me think "How can people be like this?".

Like we did before, let's go through the types of abuse here and then the tools and techniques.

Verbal abuse, mental abuse, emotional abuse, sexual abuse. These are all here.

Verbal abuse – talking to someone like that. Swearing, talking aggressively, rudeness.

Mental abuse - trying to convince someone that what they saw, and thought was a lie. It messes with people's heads and makes them doubt their own sanity. We'll talk more about this now with the tools and techniques.

Emotional abuse – comparing the situation to his ex cheating on him, making him feel like he isn't enough, making him trust less. These are all related to emotional abuse, and this man has had his emotions affected for a long time from this.

Sexual abuse – this isn't just about doing something sexual to someone, it is also about using sex or sexual things to abuse someone, just like she did with what she said here:

"First off, I'll talk to whoever the fuck I want, about anything I fucking want. And secondly if I want to go and fuck every guy on there I will. You work with women every day. Maybe I should go and fuck those guys, teach you a lesson."

Now for the tools and techniques.

Gaslighting is a big one here, and I want to take some time to go into it a bit, as it is such a big tool of the abuser/narcissist. We saw it in the first story, where she tried to convince him that he had actually attacked her, and we are seeing it here by her saying he made it up and there were no messages. Without going into a massive definition of gaslighting, it is loosely defined as manipulating someone into questioning their own perception of reality. Gaslighting is basically a way for your abuser to make you doubt your own mind.

Criticism again as well, telling him he is a problem because his ex cheated too.

Blame shifting deluxe – firstly making the problem that he found the messages, like that is worse than the messages themselves. Then blaming him saying it is his fault. To a narcissist, they can cheat, have affairs, do and say whatever they want, but it is never their fault, it's yours, and if they do ever do anything that they may partially admit was wrong, they will say that they did it because you made them do it, they had no choice.

The Sledgehammer – I covered this in my previous book, but it's what I refer to as a wrecking ball, something said or done that is designed to cause maximum damage. And when she said what she said about what she plans to do, that's a Sledgehammer:

"First off, I'll talk to whoever the fuck I want, about anything I fucking want. And secondly if I want to go and fuck every guy on there I will. You work with women every day. Maybe I should go and fuck those guys, teach you a lesson."

It's interesting to see that one thing that she said can cover so many tools and abuse types, like the Sledgehammer and Sexual Abuse.

My opinion, thoughts, advice, or tips

My opinions are obviously that this is not a very nice person. I, unfortunately, think that this sounds all to familiar from many male victims that I have spoken to, and many female victims that I have spoken to as well. It seems that cheating is all to common, and that reacting like this when caught out is also too common.

In terms of advice or tips, you are going to hear the same one a lot throughout this book, as well as different ones depending on the story, but to repeat what we said in the first story – evidence, evidence, evidence. It's hard to think that you have to live that way, taking the time whenever something happens to document it, take pictures, keep records, but it is so so necessary, and so beneficial in the long run. If he had taken some pictures of the messages, then the gaslighting defence could have been countered, at least a bit. The problem with a narcissist is that they aren't rational. So even if he had shown her the pictures of the messages, she probably would have had something else lined up, like "You photoshopped those, those aren't mine, why are you starting a witch hunt?". But it would have helped years later when he was getting divorced, especially if he had evidence of the other times she was using the dating apps as well.

29

Another bit of evidence that would have been good, is if he had voice recorded the confrontation when he asked her about the messages for the first time. With a narcissist, you know that they are going to react terribly if you confront them with something, and that reaction is good evidence. Again, it's hard to think like this and live like this when you are in it, especially if you havent figured out what's going on yet, and again, you aren't collecting evidence to make your abuser see the truth - they won't - you are collecting it for court, police, friends etc. later down the line.

The last piece of advice I gave the storyteller here (and this is something I tell everyone, and I am huge believer in), is to go and get some counselling. There are plenty of things to get counselling for once you have been in an abusive relationship, but from this story I recommended talking to someone about his lack of trust, and about how he believed the lies his abuser told him that it was him making her cheat. He has to learn to hear his own voice again, and not his abuser's voice when it comes to relationships. I was cheated on, and I know exactly what he was going through and how he felt, but with help and time you can overcome those doubts.

Chapter 3: Hulk Smash

This story also comes from a man who was married to his abuser. This didn't even happen at home; they were away in another city staying at a Bed & Breakfast for a few days. The abuse was already underway by this point obviously, and things had been escalating, from just verbal, to some physical, loads of emotional/mental, and, as we'll see, bigger blow ups by his abuser.

Let's jump right in.

The Story

We had gone away for a few days to another city, about a 2-hour flight from where we lived. I didn't really want to go, as things were just getting worse and worse with her blow ups, her rudeness, and she was getting more and more aggressive. It was to go to her relative's wedding, so I didn't really have much of a say.

We were staying in a bed and breakfast, and we had our own little flat with a kitchen, lounge, bedroom and bathroom, so we weren't sharing any spaces with other guests. The other flats were on top of us though, so I guess they would have been able to hear things that happened.

Anyway, one of the big things that she always used to go on and on about, was that I had a lock on my phone, so it needed my thumb print to open it. I literally just had it there for security, as a lot of my work stuff was on the phone, like emails, apps etc. I wasn't locking it for any bad reasons, and certainly wasn't talking to other women or anything like that (I found out later that she was doing stuff like that, maybe that's why she was so over the top about it).

We got there on the Thursday afternoon, and the wedding was on the Saturday. We were going to meet up on the Friday with some of her other family members who had travelled for it for some lunch.

That night when we were lying in bed, it was the usual demand to see my phone, because I was on it. To be clear, I was on my phone checking emails, scrolling through random videos, and playing a little bubble breaker type game that I found entertaining. That's pretty much all I did on my phone, besides checking football scores when matches were on, if my team was playing.

I gave her the phone, and grabbed a book, because I knew this would be a few hours of forensically going through my phone trying to find anything she could, and even though there was nothing to find, I knew she would have something to say about something. She always did, and it was always nothing, like the time she wanted to know why I commented "Happy Birthday" on a woman's Facebook page, and it was my cousin. She literally had the same surname as us for God's sake.

After about 40 minutes of searching, reading every message, every email, everything, she "found it". She wanted to know why I told a female colleague that they were a rock star. I very calmly explained that if she scrolled down in the mail trail, she would see that I had asked one of the ladies who reported to me to do a massive task and it was very last minute and a tonne of work. She delivered it on time and great quality, and so I said "Thanks, you're a rock star!". That was it. Five words, but a problem for her apparently. At length I was told how that is clearly flirting, and I knew what I was doing. I told her I didn't know that was flirting, I was praising a colleague for doing good work, and it was part of being a manager. After a while, and many apologies from me, she let it drop and we went to sleep. I hoped that was the end of that, and the weekend wouldn't be more of this, but I didn't get what I hoped for.

The next morning, we got up and had some breakfast that I made. She stayed in bed; I made tea and breakfast in bed for her. Not the main thing here, but whenever I made breakfast in bed for her, she would complain about how I didn't ask her first, and I was trying to tell her what she was allowed to have for breakfast. I was always just trying to do something nice to avoid getting crapped on all day.

It was after breakfast that the real trouble began. I waited for her to shower first and come out, and then I went to the toilet, and I took my phone with me so that I could watch mindless videos while on the toilet, something I did all the time. I went in, locked the door, and went about my business.

Within about 30 seconds she was absolutely hammering on the door, demanding to know why I had taken my phone in with me. I told her why, but she was having none of it, insisting I was up to no good. I told her she was being ridiculous, which apparently was not the right thing to say, and she started hitting the door harder and harder. I told her to stop because she was going to damage it and I would have to pay for it to be fixed, and the neighbouring guests would hear.

About ten seconds later the wooden frame where the door lock was split and broke, and she was in the bathroom. She snatched my phone off of me, and I obviously couldn't get up and do anything as I was "pre-occupied" on the toilet. I was rushing to finish up so I could get off the toilet and she started screaming. When she had snatched the phone, she must have hit the button on the side, so it locked. She was accusing me of locking it deliberately so that she couldn't read whatever I was doing.

I was mad at this point, this was so ludicrous, I couldn't even go to the toilet without being wrong. I told her that. Wrong thing again. She was screaming, demanding I unlock the phone with my fingerprint. I told her no unless she calmed down. Triple wrong thing to say.

She threw my phone as hard as she could on to the floor and started stamping on it, picking it back up and throwing it down, stamping some more. It was literally smashed to bits.

Apparently if she couldn't have access to it, no one could. I was told then and there that she would be going for out for the day without me (which I was actually pretty happy with), and she got her bag and the rental car keys and left. I had to pay for damages obviously for the door and lock that were broken when we checked out.

It wasn't the last time she smashed a phone of mine, and after that she even smashed two laptops.

When I did get a new phone eventually (I couldn't afford a new one right away), she made me add her fingerprint onto it so that she could unlock it whenever she wanted.

Towards the end of our relationship, when I was starting to try and get out of it, she would often grab my phone when I wasn't looking and it was unlocked and add her fingerprint back, because I had removed it.

That relationship went on for seven more years after that day. Seven. I feel ashamed of myself for that.

The Unpacking

When you can't even go to the toilet without getting abused, it's bad. This was bad before he even got to the toilet part, but it just kept getting worse. It still amazes me, but doesn't surprise me anymore, that people who are up to no good on their phones, are so controlling of their partner's phones. I assume it's because they think that everyone is like them and obviously cheating.

So, for the types of abuse in this story we have - emotional, verbal, mental, and physical.

Verbal abuse is easy, because she was talking to him like he was rubbish, accusing him of ridiculous things he wasn't doing, and she could see for herself on his phone that he wasn't.

Emotional and mental abuse, because he was already ground into submission, knowing what was going to happen before it even did. He lived in fear of outbursts, couldn't even relax in bed on his phone, and couldn't even go the toilet in peace. Permanently walking on eggshells is how he described it to me. Abusers do this to make it easier to manipulate you, by being able to trigger your emotions with behaviours or phrases that they know will rock you and get the emotional response that they can then use against you.

Physical abuse - she didn't hit him or attack him but breaking a door open and ripping something out of someone's hand, and then smashing it to pieces qualifies in my opinion. They were physical acts of domination and control.

37

Tools and Techniques.

Fear obviously. He was terrified of her reactions to everything, and of her outbursts that he even said just got worse each time. She was getting more and more comfortable acting however she wanted.

Blame shifting again. He was at fault for using his phone. He was at fault for having female coworkers. She wasn't at fault for demanding access to his phone.

Gaslighting again too. Trying to make him think that calling a staff member a rock star is flirting, so that he doubts himself, is definitely gaslighting.

Isolation. She did something terrible, and then left him without a phone or car. She didn't want to risk that he said something to her family at lunch, so she left him with no contact. He did tell me that when she came home, she told him he better not say anything about it. Undoubtedly at lunch with her family she did some pre-empting too, blaming him and making up a different story in which she was the victim.

I'd say breaking the door open while he was on the toilet qualifies for the Sledgehammer too. Pretty big event and big actions from an abuser.

My opinion, thoughts, advice, or tips

Have you ever thought to yourself "someone is telling me they got accosted while on the toilet, and they want my advice?" No, probably not. I never thought I would ever be asked that, but here we are.

In this whole story, there isn't really that much to advise on or give tips on that are going to stop the abuse. A lot of people who might hear this story and don't understand abuse or narcissists will probably be asking the dreaded question "Why didn't you just leave them?" If you are asking that, please please please go and read my previous book, handily titled "Why didn't you just leave them? And other ignorant things people say about abusive relationships" because it is not anywhere near as easy as that. It's not that he didn't want to leave, he couldn't. Take my word for that.

Advice I can give is similar to some you have read before in the first few stories.

Keep evidence. Harder here given his phone had been smashed to bits, so he couldn't exactly take pictures, but he could have spoken to a neighbour to get pictures taken and emailed to him (probably not though as he would have been too embarrassed), and he could have kept the receipts for the damages he had to pay. They wouldn't prove abuse, but they would be something to add in to more evidence bundles later when he eventually left. There can be no blame laid at the feet of victims for not collecting this kind of evidence, as how are they to know? Why would you have full knowledge of narcissism and abuse if you havent had experience with it in some way or another? That's a big part of why I am writing books on these topics, to hopefully give people the knowledge they need upfront, so that they can avoid years and years of this.

Back down. Horrible to keep having to say this, but this can actually be a piece of advice that can save your life or prevent serious harm. Apologise even when you don't need to, don't argue back, and try to learn your abusers' behaviours to avoid repercussions (like not taking your phone into the toilet with you). I hate having to write this, as it is so unfair, but this is the real world and it's far from a perfect one, sometimes you have to just survive, and sometimes to survive, you have to do things that make you feel sick afterwards. You aren't weak for doing it, you shouldn't be ashamed or embarrassed, you are stronger than most people will know for being able to survive.

Last piece of advice for this story, and for the man brave enough to tell it. I told him something that he had a hard time believing, as most male survivors do, and I certainly did for a long long time – do not feel ashamed. You have nothing to be ashamed of. You don't ever watch the news, see that someone was killed, and say "oh they got killed, they should be ashamed of themselves!". The only person who needs to feel ashamed is your abusive narcissist, but the sad harsh truth of it is, they won't. But just because they won't, doesn't mean you should. People said this to me too when I first got out of my abusive relationship, and I couldn't take it in. I was ashamed, I was embarrassed, I was humiliated. But something changed over time, and it changed because I learnt more and more about abusers and narcissists, I went to counselling for what had happened to me, and I spoke to others like me who had suffered at the hands of someone else. And over time, I learnt the truth about the abusers, what they are and how they operate, and how sophisticated they are with their techniques of abuse. As they say, the truth will set you free. Once you know the truth, you can forgive yourself, and understand that the blame is not yours. I hope every survivor can know that truth one day.

Chapter 4: Show me the money!

This story is from a man who, by this point, was married to his abuser for a few years already. They had two children, he was working in very senior roles in the corporate world, and he was the sole bread winner for the family. This isn't one incident, but a series of multiple incidents around the same thing, and the lasting impact it had on his mindset when it came to work. He said the incidents started earlier, but he only recognised the pattern when they got more serious and blatant.

The Story

I always had good jobs. From when I first met her, to when we got divorced, I always had top jobs in the corporate world, and made good money. I know now that no matter how much I ever earned, it would never have been enough for her. But that's not how I always thought.

I'll start with the first time I remember it coming up, and then move through the years to the last few times it happened, which actually go beyond our divorce.

The first time I recall was when we weren't even married yet. We were living together and had just bought our first house together. I had started a new job, and she had just decided she wasn't going to work anymore. I remember that she just decided that on her own one day. No discussions, she just stopped working. I've always been one to think that it's my role as a man to provide, and I must work hard to make sure we have everything, and obviously she knew that, and used that against me a lot.

I had been with the job a couple of weeks only, and it was very much "thrown in at the deep end" kind of stuff, so I was leaving early for work, and getting home probably around 7pm most nights. It was just the 2 of us, we didn't have any children. She started to make comments at first, about how she thought I'd be home earlier, and it was more senior so I wouldn't have to work as hard. I'd say it doesn't work that way, I have a big team now I am responsible for, and there is so much to do to fix problems that were happening, and that was one of the reasons they hired me in the first place. To put it into context as well, I was getting paid about 30% more than I was at my previous job, so I was very pleased with that. I also was only getting home an hour later than I usually did only, so it wasn't like I was working until midnight every night.

Her comments soon turned into statements like "If you are working so hard and fixing their mess, they should be paying you way more", to then "you need to talk to your boss and tell him you want a raise". That was about 4 weeks into the new job. I told her I can't do that; I've just started, I need to prove my worth first, I can't ask for a raise immediately. She very much played on the angle of how they are taking advantage of me, and how I am worth more, and how I am meant to be providing for us, and coming home "so late" should be rewarded. I spoke to my boss but was so shy and embarrassed about it. He said the same thing I did, that I had just started and had to prove my worth, and they don't do pay rises out of the performance review cycles anyway. She was not happy with that answer, but didn't say much else, so I thought maybe she would leave it. She didn't. She started to send me job listings for jobs that paid more, and for agencies that could place me at other jobs. She insisted I move jobs because I should be getting paid more. All while this was happening, her best friend and her husband had just bought a really nice house, so she was obviously jealous and comparing, even though their circumstances were so different to ours. This would be a theme as our relationship went on. She always compared our life to someone else, but it was never apples with apples.

I moved jobs after a few more months, got paid more, it wasn't enough. That cycle repeated quite a few times. No matter what I got paid, she would say it should be more. No matter what we had, we should have more. It got worse and worse, and became mixed in with other types of abuse, like her telling me I was a failure, didn't provide properly for our family, wasn't as good as her friend's husbands etc. The one thing I always thought was "funny", is that the husbands she would compare me to earned about the same as me, or in some cases slightly less, but the wife also worked, so they had double income. We didn't, it was just me providing. While all of this was happening, she also "took charge" of all of our finances, meaning she took my salary, and "managed it", which loosely put was her taking what she wanted and giving me the bare minimum of my own money to use on things for me, or just plain telling me I wasn't allowed to buy things.

There's no point going into every single job move I made, but there are two more examples I think are good to tell. One is the job I had before we got divorced, and the other is the one I got after we were divorced.

Before we were divorced, I was in a very senior role in one of the top companies in its industry. It was a great role, paid well, and I was learning so much. This time, the hours were long. We were working on a very big piece of work, that was all consuming. It meant getting to work early, and often working late.

Because of where the office was and where we lived, it took me about an hour by trains and walking to get there, so if I left the office at 7PM, I wouldn't get home until at least 8PM, if I caught the trains on time. She saw the lifestyle my boss was living (holidays all of the time, a driver, fancy apartment in the city etc.) and she decided we should have the same, even though he had 25 years more experience than me and was at the top of his career. She told me I WILL talk to him and tell him I need more. I hate conversations like that, they make me so uncomfortable, but I did as I was told. He agreed that I did deserve more and said he would look into it. About a week later, he told me that would be upping my salary by 20%, which I thought was fantastic. She did not. She wanted more. She wasn't working at all, the kids were at a very nice school, and we had a very nice house. She would constantly tell me how I should tell him I want more, but there was no way I could do that, I was worried I would be fired or knock myself off the fast-track I was on. As the work got to the last few months of where we were going to close it out, it got more intense, and the late nights were more and more frequent. This got her to push even harder, and between her trying to convince me that I was getting screwed over, and that I was a failure as a provider, I decided I would talk to the boss. Surprisingly, he was ok with the conversation, probably because I was really going above and beyond, and he depended on me so much. Same as before, he said he would come back to me. When he did, it was with a massive raise, like 35%, but also with a very serious "we aren't going to have this conversation again any time soon" message. I was really happy with the raise, but also a little pissed off that he obviously knew I was worth way more but wasn't giving it to me without me asking, but I guess that's just the corporate world for you. Money wise, I was ecstatic though, it was so much more money, and I felt great about it. Until I told her about it. I got the usual diatribe about how it wasn't enough; I should be getting what he is getting (which was more than double what I was getting), and how I can't even provide properly. That was the last time a raise or job moved was discussed while we were "together" because a few months after that I moved out and started divorce proceedings, not just because of this, but because of all of the other abuse I suffered daily.

About six months after we got divorced, I got a new job, and this was the big one. A top top job, something I had worked my whole life towards, and the pay was amazing. As I was paying for the children, and we were still in financial proceedings to agree a monthly maintenance payment for her and the kids, she got to know what my salary was. Amazingly, she wanted to still tell me that it wasn't enough, and that given my role, I should demand more. The audacity of this greedy woman, I couldn't quite believe it. As it was most of my salary was going to her and the kids anyway while we sorted out the legal proceedings, and she was wasting it faster than I could earn it with fancy meals out, trips away, coffees everyday with friends etc, and conversely, I was living a very meagre life, just working. Through every single legal proceeding, and every single financial discussion after that she just came with greed, greed, and more greed. It was so bad, that one day when I dropped the kids at hers after my weekend with them, she commented on how the t-shirt I was wearing was new, and clearly, I was spending money on myself that could go to her. Not that it matters where my t-shirt was from, or how much it cost, but it was literally from the cheapest store around and cost less than one of her fancy coffees she had daily. She had taken so much from me, and in the divorce took even more, but it still wasn't enough. It never would be.

The Unpacking

While he was telling me his story, it had so many similarities to my own, and I knew the torment he would have gone through with this kind of abuse. Never being enough is so soul destroying. You work hard, you get more, but no matter what, it will never be enough to get anything other than abuse and scorn from a narcissist.

There are various types of abuse here that are similar to others we have seen in the stories before this one, like verbal, emotional, and mental abuse, but the big new one at play here is financial abuse. Let's focus in on that one, as it is so prevalent in narcissistic/abusive relationships and can be so damaging for the victim long term in terms of their financial well being and how they can get on with life once they are free of the relationship.

I'll take a little excerpt from my previous book around financial control:

"Abusers and narcissists love financial control. Taking control over your money to force you to rely on them, or to prevent you from getting things. By taking away or altering your financial freedom, they can control you further, make it harder for you to build self-worth, and manipulate your behaviours. With most narcissists, they believe that they are owed everything, and so it's not just about preventing you from having the money, it's about getting it for themselves. They then not only have the control, but they can also use the finances as they see fit, and have everything that they want, while preventing you from having anything. It's a win-win for them."

Couple the above with the fact that she was constantly telling him he wasn't good enough or providing enough, and it's easy to see how he was being forced to try and get more and more, and it was all so that she could take more and more. It was never about her feeling that he was not being treated fairly by his employers, it was always just about what she could get.

In terms of tools and techniques, we have some recurring ones, like criticism. Abusers will always criticise, as it's an easy way for them to break down your spirit and make you more vulnerable to their abuse.

Triangulation – she introduced an enemy, his boss at every job he was at, to play off of. The boss was bad, and she was helping him combat the injustice of his unfair salary. Narcissists do this to try and strengthen your link to them, because they pretend that they have your best interests at heart.

My opinion, thoughts, advice, or tips

I went through something similar, and I didn't do anything different than he did at the time. I didn't know about narcissists properly then, and I didn't understand all of the types of abuse, or tools and techniques.

Realistically, I don't think I would have done anything differently in the situation, and I didn't think he could have either, because in order to do something differently, you would have to understand what it is you are dealing with.

What I discussed with him in terms of advice was something a little different. We spoke about what advice we could give to someone before they get into a relationship, that could help them avoid this kind of thing. Arm people up front with the knowledge so to speak.

Obviously if people can learn about the different forms of abuse, learn about narcissism, learn about the tools and techniques of an abuser early on in adulthood, that's great, because they might see the warning signs a lot earlier than we did. But besides telling people to learn, what else can we give them advice on.

I have a practical exercise I think is good for this kind of thing, and can help in various ways, but can really help you keep focus on your core beliefs, to make sure that they aren't getting overridden by an abuser's wants.

Write down what kind of a person you are deep down, and the type of person you want to be. What are your beliefs and values? Do you think money is the most important thing in the life? Do you think job happiness is important or only your salary? Does making more money make you happy? Do you have to keep up with the Jones', or are you happy to go your own path?

By doing this, it can form a good blueprint for the way you will think about things as you progress throughout your career. Refer back to it when you are thinking of moving jobs or looking at career changes. I worked in the corporate work myself for 20+ years, and I really wish that I had received this advice before I began. To me now, life is about begin happy, and while having money is great, and working hard is great, there is so much more to it, and I wish I realised that all of those years ago.

Chapter 5: It wasn't me

This story was from a man in a long-term relationship. They weren't married but had been together for 9 years and had 3 children together. He said that verbal/emotional/mental abuse had been going on for about 4 years, and physical for about 2. He did admit to me though, he wasn't sure if the abuse had started earlier and he just didn't recognise until it became "obvious", as he put it. This is another man who did not fit the "typical physical profile" for an abuse victim, so I have included his size below. This story is a little longer, and the unpacking is too, as it has something very important that I would like to highlight.

The Story

Height: 6 foot 2 inches

Weight: 100kg/220lbs

This was one of the biggest blow ups, incidents, fights, whatever you want to call it, we had in our relationship. I can't remember what started it, I can't remember what started any of them really as it was always something whether big or small that set her off, but I remember what happened and how it "ended".

I do remember it was a Saturday, and it started in the morning. The usual arguments, followed by screaming, yelling, and being put down constantly. What wasn't usual was the degree the physical stuff escalated to, and how quickly it escalated. The constant commentary and stream of expletives as coming from the living room, and I was in the hallway downstairs busy putting up a picture with nails. Downstairs was just the living room, a hallway, the kitchen, and a toilet, then the stairs went upstairs where the bedrooms were and where the kids were all playing.

I honestly have no idea what she was saying, or what it was even about, I pretty much was at the point where I just zoned out whenever she started one of her rants. They were juvenile, pointless, and just designed to try and get a reaction from me, and to hurt me as much as she could during them with what she would say.

I was busy putting the frame on the nail, trying to get it centred, when next thing I knew I was being hit. She had hit me plenty of times before, but it usually built up to that, not just straight into hitting from ranting in another room.

I let go of the picture frame, and luckily it was on the nail, so it didn't fall and smash. I backed away and covered up to stop the hits, but she kept swinging, and her punches were hitting the top of my left arm and my shoulder. She was much smaller than me, but when she punched, it really hurt. I kept backing off and got to the kitchen, and I ducked inside to get a break from the blows.

The other really strange thing was that she was saying nothing, just attacking. Usually it was a screaming, swearing, spitting rage along with hits, but this was just an attack. Normally it would be hitting with a verbal demand, like apologise for something or say something she wanted to hear in order to get the hitting to stop, but this was very different. She kept punching and I kept backing away, covered up, until I got to the back of the kitchen and had nowhere else to go. She hit me a few more times, and then she took a step back. I hoped that was it, but I then very quickly realised she had backed away so that she could get close enough to the drawers to open one up and come out with a kitchen knife. It wasn't the biggest carving knife in the world, but the blade was about 3 inches long and certainly enough to do some serious damage. She was just standing there with it out in front of her, and she finally spoke. All I got was a "I'm going to fucking kill you!", and she came forward.

As she got close to me, she had her arm out in front of her holding the knife, so I grabbed her wrist. I'm much stronger than she is, so I knew she wouldn't be able to break my grip. She was slapping at my head with her left hand, trying to get me to let go. I didn't, I just held it and tried to move her around so that I could get out of the door and her be with her back to the wall. When she was moved around, and I had my back to the door, and she was up against the back wall of the kitchen, I pushed her wrist back, probably hard enough to knock a coke can off a table, but not hard enough to even close a car door, and she went straight from standing there with a knife to being in Hollywood. She threw herself backwards into the wall and dived onto the floor like she had just been tackled in the box and was trying to win the World Cup winning penalty. It was so ridiculous. Like bad wrestling acting. She rolled around on the floor for a second, so I just turned and walked out of the kitchen. She shook off her stupid act and came straight back for more, with the knife in hand again. I backed away into the downstairs toilet and was telling her to stop. She started screaming at me about how I had attacked her. What the fuck! She was literally trying to stab me, after hitting me, and now she wanted to go with the story of me attacking her. I thought maybe she had lost her mind, but figured out later why that she was saying it loudly so that the neighbours might hear her "version".

She kept trying to get to me with the knife, but I had hold of her wrist again. By this stage I had had enough. She was being insane, she was screaming, she had hurt me, and was now using a knife against me. I grabbed her hand and started to bend her fingers off the knife. She dropped it very quickly, and I kept bending her fingers. By now she was realising the pain in her hand was bad and was telling me to stop. I told her if she ever tried to come at me with a knife again, I would break her fingers. I was so mad.

Right at that moment, our one child walked in and saw me bending her hand and her in pain, so they cried at me to stop. They had missed all of her attacking me but saw that one thing. I know they would have heard her and had seen her attack me plenty of times before, but it still hurt me because I wasn't the aggressor and so didn't want to be seen by my own kid as such. I let go immediately, and was caught off guard again when, rather than stop as our kid was there, she bent down, grabbed the knife back up and waved it at me telling me if I ever touched her again, she would cut my throat. She stormed off to the kitchen, threw the knife on the counter, walked into the hallway, paused long enough to smash the framed picture I had just hung up, and marched off upstairs.

I checked my kid was okay, told them it was all ok and it was just a silly argument, and they could go and play on their video games in their room, because I had to clean up the glass and didn't want them to cut themselves.

I was on my knees getting the glass into a dustpan with the little brush when she came back downstairs, grabbed one of the shards, and said she was going to kill herself. All very matter of fact, and the usual ending to one of her big episodes. She would lock herself in the bathroom "threatening" suicide until I apologised and begged for her not to.

The ending to this one was going to be different though, and I quickly realised it when the doorbell sounded. I opened the door to find two police officers standing there. We lived in a terrace house, and the neighbours had heard her screaming, and had rung the police. They asked me where she was, and I told them she was in the bathroom, threatening to kill herself, and so one of the officers went upstairs, and the other radioed in for some more help, and took me into the kitchen to sit down and explain what was happening. For the first time, I told someone everything that had happened. I didn't hold back, try and protect her, nothing. I just told him what had happened. I showed him the broken picture, the knife, the red marks across my head, the marks on my arms from being punched, and told him exactly what she had done and said. I told him what I had done to her fingers, and what I had said to her about breaking them.

He listened and wrote everything down on his little machine he had with him. He left me at the table and went off to chat to his colleague who was dealing with her. By this stage, there was another pair of officers there, and they were both upstairs too, one with the colleague and her, and one standing in the passageway, just making sure the children were staying in their rooms.

He came back a little while later, I have no idea if it was five minutes or fifty, but when he did come back, he told me that they were arresting her and taking her with them. He asked if I was ok to be there with the children and told me that someone would call me later from the station. I was scared. I asked him what happens when she comes back home, and I asked what was going to happen to the kids. She had me convinced that if anything ever got said about how she behaved that the kids would be taken away. He gave me some sort of generic reply about taking one step at a time, and that someone would contact me to discuss everything. With that they all left, taking her with them.

I spent the rest of the late afternoon with the kids, making sure they were ok, and getting them dinner and ready for bed. Once they were all in bed, I went and lay down and started Googling about what would happen to the kids now. Would they be taken away? Would they go to a foster home? I had no idea.

About 9PM I got the first call from the police. The lady explained that they had her at the station, and were taking her statement, and going through all the procedures they have to. She told me the kids would not be taken away, but that a social worker would have to come and talk to us and do checks on them. The main thing she wanted to know is if I would be willing to take things further and have formal charges laid against her. I didn't know. I was scared of what would happen, of what that meant of the kids, and of the repercussions. I told her that and she said to think about it, and she would ring me later. She rang me back about 11:30PM and said that they were going to have to let her go as her story was very different to mine and there was no evidence besides the marks on me. She said they would take it further if I was willing to provide another statement and if I could provide evidence (of which I had plenty by that point), but I only had 72 hours to decide, otherwise they would close the file on it. I said I'd think about it. She told me that they would be letting her go in an hour or so, but she had been told to not come back to the house that night. That was something at least.

I couldn't sleep, and about 2AM my phone pinged, and I had a message from her friend, asking me to pack a bag of her toiletries and some clothes for a few days, and that she was fetching her from the station and would take her in for a few days. I packed it, and left it on the doorstep, and told her she could just grab it there.

Sunday was a complete blur, the kids and I stayed home and watched movies I think, but Monday had more in store. I had already told my boss that I couldn't come to work for a few days as we had a stomach bug outbreak at home (I obviously wasn't going to tell him the truth about what happened), and that morning I took the kids to school. When I was walking back to the car after dropping them, her friend was waiting there for me (her kids went to the same school). She said she didn't want to get involved with what "I had done" (so the stories had obviously been flowing about how I was the monster, and the real abuser was the helpless victim), but that they had been talking and they were worried that the kids were going to be taken away if I didn't drop everything with the police, because that's what happened. I told her that the police told me that wasn't going to happen, but she said that the police always say that to get you to talk more, but then you lose your kids. I was shaken, and I didn't know what to believe. When I got home, I called the policewoman back and told her I won't take it further. She was disappointed, but said she understood. To this day I still wonder if she did understand or not.

Fast forward to the next day, and she returned home. She was furious that I had "called the police" even though I kept explaining that I didn't. All she cared about was how she now looked to her and friend and her husband. She had stayed with them, so she had told them her version of events. Her story was basically how I had attacked her, how I had smashed the picture, threatened to kill her, and then bent her fingers and hurt her. She had told them that the police had taken her away because I had lied about everything. As if it wasn't enough that she had lied to them (which I knew she would obviously), she then demanded that I create a WhatsApp group chat with her, her friend, and her friend's husband, and apologise to them for the hassle I had caused with my terrible actions, and basically take all of the blame and back up her version of events. I'm still embarrassed to this day about it, but I did. I took the blame for it all and apologised to them for "my inexcusable behaviour". The only good thing was that the next time we saw the friend, the husband took me aside and said he knew that my message my bullshit and that I was taking the blame for what she had done. That made me feel a little bit better at least.

For years following that incident, while we were still together and after, she still stuck to her version of events. It's like she had convinced herself that her story was really what happened.

The Unpacking

There's an awful lot to unpack here. Different types of abuse, and different tools and technique used by his abuser. I'm going to touch on them briefly, because there is something very important to talk about on the back of this story.

For types of abuse we have verbal, physical, mental, and emotional. For the tools and techniques, we have fear, manipulation, gaslighting, isolation, the Sledge Hammer, pre-empting, and blame shifting. I'll cover off bits of these in the opinion/advice section below, but first let's look at a very big item.

Some people think that people who are being abused just take it. That they get hit, verbally abused, spat on, slapped, and more, and never lose their tempers, never say anything back, or do anything back to their abusers. That is not the case. And, even worse, some people think that if you do say or do anything back, then "you are just as bad as each other". WRONG!

This is something I discussed with this storyteller – the fact that he had retaliated. He was really upset and conflicted about it. He felt that it made him just as bad as her, and that he was a hypocrite. I'll try and summarise here what I told him.

There is a very big difference between constantly abusing someone, and eventually having enough of the abuse and retaliating. I don't condone physical violence at all, but if you are being attacked and your life threatened, and you have to defend yourself, then I'd say that it's understandable if you do something physical in return. Even if you remove the physical stuff, if someone is constantly running you down, verbally abusing you, swearing at you, belittling you, and one day you have had enough and say something back, or call them something terrible, you can't equate that to what they are doing.

Obviously, you need to be careful that it doesn't become an excuse for saying and doing whatever you want, because that is exactly what a narcissist does. They do and say whatever they feel like, and then say that you "made them" do it.

One of the worst things about retaliation when you are in a relationship with a narcissist, is that your retaliation becomes fodder for their abuse machine. They will focus on what you did, make you apologize, constantly bring it up, and use it to blame shift, by saying you are the abuser and not them. When you do get out of the relationship, that will be the main thing they tell everyone else – the times you retaliated will now be stories of the times you abused them.

It's the sad, unfortunate reality of a relationship with a narcissist – you cannot win, no matter what you do. All you can do is try to get out, do damage limitation, and try to move on far away from their hate and lies.

My opinion, thoughts, advice, or tips

So, my opinions that I gave the storyteller are pretty much what I said above. He isn't a monster for retaliating, he isn't also an abuser, and he isn't "just as bad as her". He is human though, and he had his limits, and she was pushing them every single day.

In terms of advice, it is so easy to give advice after the fact, when you aren't in the situation. You can say all the obvious things like "you should have left the house and gone for a walk or something", but then what about the children being left alone with someone raging? You could say "you should have pressed charges with the police" but then what about his fear of the children being taken away?

When you are in a situation, it is very difficult to act perfectly, and to do exactly the right thing for both short term and long term. Abused people learn how to respond to minimise the abuse they receive, and it may work well for the short term, but long term it doesn't, and vice versa, you may do something for the long term that will result in more abuse now.

So, for any situation that has happened, my advice will be similar – document them, keep evidence, and do it safely.

For people who havent had the situations yet, and want to avoid them in life altogether, the advice is fairly consistent too. Learn. Read, listen, understand, and educate yourself about these topics so that you don't have to learn through experience. It's one of life's terrible ironies, that you can't fully understand it without experiencing it, but a bit of knowledge around it will hopefully let you go into any relationship with your eyes wide open.

Chapter 6: This little piggy went to hospital

This story actually comes from a man who had already left and divorced his abuser, but he wasn't out of the abuse fully yet. She still had control of him. After they had separated, and he had moved out, he was fetching the children from school three times a week and taking them home to her place. She had him coming into the house, and doing her laundry, dishes, and gardening though, claiming that it was "for the children" and that "every man did the same" after divorce.

Obviously, that is not the case at all, and she was using him, and so this story is about when he realised that and was going to tell her that he wasn't doing it anymore.

The Story

I was fetching the kids from school three times a week, and taking them back to hers, which was 5 minutes from school, but 35 minutes from my new place where I was staying. She didn't work, but she also wouldn't lift a finger to do anything herself if she could help it. On the days I fetched the kids, I was expected to bring them home, come into the house to spend time with the kids, but also do all the housework and chores. I had to put laundry on, hang it up when it was done to dry, fold away stuff that was dry from the time before, pack it into the cupboards, unpack the dishwasher and reload it, and if the lawn needed mowing or weeding I had to do that too, although that wasn't every time obviously, and then whatever else needed doing like bins taking out and so on. So, from about 3:30PM onwards I was doing stuff with the kids like board games, video games, games outside, but in between having to stop to sort laundry and do the other chores. Then as it got to about 7:30PM I had to get the kids sorted for bed (showered, teeth brushed etc.), make sure they had everything ready for school the next day, and then put them to bed with a bedtime story. When that was all done, at around 8:15PM, I could leave. So, I would get home just before 9PM on those nights, and then sort myself out some dinner and whatever I needed to do at my place.

Once or twice, I had mentioned that I didn't think this was right, and that this set up was a bit weird, we were divorced, and I was still there doing the housework. This was always shut down quickly and aggressively (like everything in our relationship was) with a "every other father does this for their kids" or "you aren't doing it for me, you are doing it for the kids" or "you did it before when you lived here so I need the help now". She didn't work and was home all day unless she was having coffee or lunch with friends, so doing some housework wouldn't have been a problem for her, but she was immensely lazy. She was still getting money from me obviously, so if I was doing the housework, then divorce wasn't bad for her, because she could just do whatever she wanted anyway.

As the weeks and months went on, I got more and more upset with this arrangement. I loved seeing my kids and spending time with them, but the ongoing abuse was what I was trying to escape when I left and got divorced in the first place. There were also other things, like her telling me they were going away for a week, and I had to housesit while they were away, look after the dog, and make sure the house was perfect for when they returned. I felt like the freedom I had fought so hard to try and win wasn't there, and that I was still in the abusive relationship (which I was, just not "formally").

One night I went out, for the first time in years, to have a beer with one of the other dads from school, and I ended up opening up a bit about it. He couldn't believe it. He said I was totally being used, and he had never heard of anyone else doing what I was doing. Divorced meant separate, not having your ex as a servant.

I made up my mind that next time I was over there I was going to tell her that this was the end of this arrangement, and that I would still fetch the kids from school, but I would take them to the park for a bit, then drop them at home with her, and I wouldn't be coming inside anymore, as it had to stop. I knew she would fight against it, as it meant losing out on her cleaner and gardener, and that she might have to actually do some work around her own house.

Next time I was round there, I got the kids in, sorted a few things, and thought I'd wait until later in the evening to talk about things. I thought she might be less volatile if a few of the chores had been done first. It didn't work out that way at all.

At about 7:20PM, just before I would usually start getting the kids ready for bed, I told her that this would be the last time. I said I was not going to come into the house anymore and do chores, but I would take the kids after school to the park for a play and then bring them home. She went absolutely berserk. She was screaming at me, telling me how I'm a pathetic father, not even willing to help his kids, and how she can't manage a house on her own, and how every other divorced dad that she knows does the same. I stood firm. I said no, they don't, and I am no longer doing it, and that's final.

70

We were in the dining room at this point, and she started throwing the chairs over. Two of them (they were plastic chairs with metal legs so not heavy) got thrown into the wall, and she was screaming the place down. I backed away to not get hit with a flying chair, and she went from full rage to dead stop within about one second. It was terrifying. She literally just stopped screaming and throwing chairs, and looked at me and said, "Where's your phone?". As part of our divorce, I had gathered evidence of her rages by using the voice recorder on my phone, so she obviously thought I was doing the same here. I wasn't, but she obviously thought I was. I told her it was in my pocket, but I wasn't recording, but she was certain this was some kind of trap. "Give me your fucking phone now!!" was all I got in return. I said no, you have no right to my phone, but I can show you I am not recording if you want. I took my phone out to try and show her that there was no recording happening, and she lunged to try and grab it from me. I pulled back and put it back in my pocket, telling her again that she could not have my phone. Being told no was all she could bare it seemed, at that sent her into an even bigger rage. She ran up to me, stamped down with all her weight as hard as she could on my right foot (I was bare foot as I always took my shoes off when I came indoors), and ran off. I was in absolute agony, sitting on the floor holding my foot, but heard the car start and her drive off. She had done that, then left. Her house. She had left me alone in her house with the kids while she left. I took a minute or two to try and breathe deeply as my foot felt like it was going to split in half, and then I got up and hobbled over to the couch in the lounge to sit down. I called to the kids, and they came into the lounge too. I told them to start getting ready for bed, and I'd be along soon to read them a story. They must have heard what had happened, but they had unfortunately seen much worse, so they didn't even say anything. I didn't know what to say, so I just said that their mother had popped out and would be back later, but I'd put them to bed and then be on the couch if they needed me.

I got the kids to bed, and their bedtime story read, and was back on the couch by about 8:25PM. I was keeping my foot up as it was throbbing so badly. It was swollen, absolutely killing, and rock hard all around my toes.

I eventually heard her car pull into the driveway closer to 10PM. I got my car keys ready, and when she came in the front door, and went to the kitchen to put her keys down, I left quickly. That was the last time I ever went into that house.

When I got home, I got an ice pack on my foot and took some anti-inflammatory tablets, hoping that it would be alright. The next day, my big toe, and the area around it was a bit bruised, nothing too bad, but it hurt a lot. The day after that however, it was purple. Like dark purple and looked horrendous. It was broken, but there wasn't a lot that could be done for it, so I had to keep it rested, iced, and give it time.

I have no idea to this day where she ran off to that night, but I assume she thought I might call the police, or something so was trying to go before I could. Who knows. I never went back in, and never did her chores again.

The Unpacking

Before we go into the unpacking of the types of abuse and the tools and techniques used, let's just take a second to highlight a really important thing that this story shows. Being "out" is a lot more than just being physically "out". Being separated, divorced, or moved out is just one piece of it, but being fully out of an abusive relationship can take time, and especially if there are children involved and you can't just get a clean break from your abuser. Even just the legal or practical side of things like divorce, child arrangement proceedings, financial maintenance proceedings and so on can take a long time to get finalised. A narcissist will try to keep their hooks into you for as long as possible, in whatever ways possible.

Let's break this story down. We have verbal abuse, emotional/mental abuse, and physical abuse. The way she screams and swears at him, the way she tries to convince him that he must do all of the chores in her house, and the physical altercation and assault. As a side note, I saw pictures of what his foot looked like in the days after the incident, and it was bad!

For tools and techniques let's talk about fear, manipulation, gaslighting, and isolation.

Fear was very clearly something used in their relationship, and it stretched beyond it too. He was scared to speak up, scared of saying no, scared of the repercussions of not doing as he was told. Even after moving out and getting divorced. The hold of fear is so strong.

Manipulation, again, was common he told me, and the way she had him doing all of the dishes, laundry, gardening and other chores just shows how much she used him.

Emotional and mental abuse in the way she tried to convince him that by not doing what she was saying meant he was a bad father, or that other men do it so he should to. The children to her are a tool here to be used against him to get what she wanted.

Isolation is worth mentioning, because it was easier for her to use and manipulate him because he didn't go out and see other people. As he told me himself, it was the first time in ages he had been out or spoken to anyone, and that wasn't by choice, it was by design from his whole relationship of being abused. Abusers want you isolated, as the less people you can speak to, the less chance they have of being caught out, and the less advice you can get to stand up to them.

I feel it's worth mentioning that none of these tools were quickly created after they got divorced, but were built up over time during their relationship, so she still had access to them. Once he put the boundaries in place of not going in the house and doing her chores for her, she had less tools to work with, and he gained back more of his own control.

An abuser/narcissist hates it when they start to lose control, so they will try and do anything to keep as much as possible.

My opinion, thoughts, advice, or tips

I was glad when he said to me about how he used voice recordings as evidence during his relationship, as from previous chapters you can see that I do believe in the importance of evidence.

My best advice I can give here for people reading this, and advice based off my own experiences of separation, divorce, legal proceedings for financials, child arrangements and more, is to get it all done as soon as possible.

What I mean by this is to get the legal things all done together if able. So don't just get divorced, because a divorce doesn't legally sort anything around child visitation rights/times etc, and it doesn't sort anything about child maintenance or spousal maintenance payments. So, you get what happened here, where he was divorced, but had nothing formally in place around the children, so it allowed her to use that against him. If you get it all done, then you have the frameworks in place to work from. It might not necessarily stop the issues fully, as abusers do what they want most of the time, but it provides you with a mechanism to challenge that, and get authorities involved if needed.

I learnt all this the hard way unfortunately, by getting divorced, and then having the child legal proceedings and financial legal proceedings go on for years after it.

The other piece of advice I can give on this is to make sure you have someone to help you with all of it, even if you don't have a lawyer. Have a friend or family member go through it all with you so that you end up with a fair arrangement. Your abuser will try and get everything, and you might be too scared to say no, so get someone to help you and make sure that doesn't happen.

Chapter 7: Flying Monkeys

This story is from another married man, and it takes place well into the heavily abusive stage of his relationship with his wife. He said that it had escalated over the previous years from verbal to physical, but at the time of this story, things just seemed to be getting worse and worse.

Size wise, this man is huge. He is tall, and built like a tank, so definitely not what most people would consider a "typical abuse victim". I really hope that people can start to see that there is no such thing as a typical abuse victim, anyone can be abused.

Before we dive into the story, let's just take a look at the chapter title – Flying Monkeys. For those who may not be fully aware, here is what Flying Monkeys means.

The term "flying monkeys" comes from the flying monkeys in The Wizard of Oz, who were sent to do the dirty work for the Wicked Witch of the West. The phrase has become used to describe people who do the bidding of a narcissist. They may even do the "bidding" unwittingly, by spreading false stories that the narcissist has told them, not realising what they are doing. They are enablers, and, unfortunately for them, pawns in the game of a narcissist. They may feel that they are friends or family, but they are really just more tools to be used. Something to realise when all is said and done, is that these people are victims too.

The Story

Height: 6 foot 2 inches

Weight: 125kg/276lbs

This story is one of my most frustrating. It wasn't the worst in terms of how badly she abused me, but I just feel it was so frustrating given how her family responded to it. I'll tell you everything that led up to the actual incident because it's all relevant, and then what happened afterwards.

We had been fighting a lot, and every fight she seemed to get more and more physical. Punching me, slapping me, hitting me with whatever was lying around. The first big fight of that day happened in the hallway, while I was walking towards the bedroom, and she was coming out of it with a plate she had used the night before and was taking to the kitchen. I have no idea how the fight started, or what it was about, or how it even escalated, but I do remember the plate being thrown at my head, but I ducked aside, and it hit the wall and broke. She was really mad that I had moved, and so she only got more angry and more aggressive. She grabbed a piece of the broken plate and started trying to stab it into me. I grabbed her arms and stopped her from being able to get the plate piece close to me, and we struggled for a bit like that. Eventually she dropped it, and when she did, I just let go and walked off. In the weeks leading up to that I had been hit a lot, with hands, fists, poles, dishes, and various other things, so I was not going to stand around and wait to be hit with more. I was about to go out anyway to grab a few things from the shop, so I just grabbed my keys and drove off.

I wasn't thinking straight at all, so I didn't know where I was going, I just wanted to not be there with her. I ended driving to a shopping centre not far from where we lived and just sitting in the carpark. I think I must have sat in the car for about an hour, just trying to breathe properly and calm my head down. I hated the fights and the attacks, they really got to me badly and made my brain feel fried. After sitting there, I decided that enough was enough, this had to stop. She was out of control, her behaviour was terrible, her attitude as disgusting, and she was only getting worse. She had been put on medication for her moods about a year before, but she refused to take them. She didn't think that she was the problem, it was everyone else. Her family had witnessed her temper on more than one occasion, and even they though never saw the full-on physical abuse, they had witnessed plenty of verbal abuse as well as complete rages. They also knew full well that she would never take responsibility, and it was always someone else's fault as to why she acted like that.

I thought that maybe if I went and spoke to them, they could help by getting her to listen to reason, see a doctor again and get on medication that might help. I rang her parents and asked if I could come over and talk to them about it.

I went over and told them what had happened that morning. They could see the scratches all up my arms from where we had struggled, and they had been witnessing her bad behaviour more and more. They agreed she was out of control, from what I told them and from what they had seen themselves. They said they had realised for a while that she needed help, and her aggression was really over the top. They thought she could do with taking something to help, and that she needed to sort herself out because she was horrible to be around for everyone. They said they hated spending time with her now, because she would always be rude, she would lose her temper, and she made them feel like rubbish.

We spoke for a long time about it, and they agreed that the best thing to do was to all sit down with her and have an open discussion, like an intervention. They had a party that they were having at their house that night, so they wanted to get that done, and then do it the next day. The suggested I go home, stay away from her, sleep in the spare room, and in the morning, they would ring her and tell her to come over for something.

I left their house with a glimmer of hope. Maybe they would help. Maybe she would listen. I didn't want to go straight home, because it was only mid-afternoon, and that would be a long time to be at home with her after what had happened that morning. She had been messaging me the whole day demanding to know where I was, but I had just ignored her. She had rung multiple times too, but I had ignored those as well. I went back to the same car park that I had sat in earlier, and tried to prepare myself mentally for what it would be like when I got home. I ordered some pizzas to collect on my way home, thinking that it might soften her reaction when I got back. I think it worked a bit, but it was more of a delay rather than a soften.

We ate separately, her in front of the tv and me in the kitchen, and then I locked up the house ready to go to bed. I grabbed a book and a glass of water and headed to the spare room to get ready for bed. She came in a few seconds later wanting to know where I had been all day. I told her I had sat in the car thinking, and I didn't want any more fights, and just wanted to go to bed, and let's talk in the morning. I was really shocked when she said OK and left the room. She never agreed with me, and certainly never tried to avoid a fight. It made me feel really uneasy actually. I finished getting ready for bed and locked myself in the spare room. I knew there was no way she could be done with everything, and I didn't want to get attacked in the night, so I made sure the door was locked, and I got into bed and began to read. It wasn't late at all; it must have been 8:30PM only. It didn't take long for her "OK" to change. She came to door and tried to open it. She obviously didn't think it was locked and wasn't happy with the fact that it was. She was now knocking on the door, telling me to open it. I told her I didn't want another fight, and I was tired, and we should go to bed and talk in the morning when we both rested and calm. She just started hitting the door harder and harder, and yelling at me louder and louder to open it. I was very firm, telling her to stop and go away and we'd talk in the morning. She didn't stop, just got louder and more enraged.

I didn't know what to do, so I rang her father. He answered and I whispered to him to listen and held the phone up. All he would have heard was the door being absolutely bashed and her screaming and swearing for me to open it. While holding the phone in front of me, I unlocked the door and opened it. I said, "here talk to your father" and tried to hand her the phone. She was shocked and confused because she had been caught out and wasn't prepared for it. She just ran off to the main bedroom. I locked the door again and told him that she had just run off. He said to go back into the spare room, lock the door and to stick to what we had agreed for the next day, and he would ring her now to try and get her to calm down. About 20 minutes later I heard the front door open and then close, and then heard her car pulling away. She had left. I messaged him to tell him that, and he said that she was coming there for the night. I thought it was a good thing, because she had been caught out, her father had heard what she was doing, and we would all talk the next day and hopefully be able to make some progress. I seriously underestimated how good a liar she was and how manipulative she could be.

In the morning, I got a message from her father saying that he was bringing her back to get a bag, and she was going to stay at their house for a few days, and to not engage with her when they got to the house. I thought everything was still good, and they had obviously spoken to her, and she was embarrassed, and we would still all talk it through. They got to the house, and I was in the garden just doing random chores. She went inside to pack, and her dad was standing by the car, so I went over to talk to him. I think I said something like "Did you talk to her? Did it go ok?" and I was absolutely floored by his response, which he practically spat at me, about how he couldn't believe I had lied to them, he was disgusted I had faked the whole thing the night before, and why was I trying to make her look bad when it was me who was the bad one and they realised that now after talking to her. Lots of things went through my head, and lots of different possible responses. Obviously, she had weaved her lies on them, and they had fallen for it, even though they had witnessed her behaviour themselves, and had heard firsthand what had happened the night before. I'm sure there were lots of things I could have said to help my case, or to get to the bottom of how they could possibly believe her, but I was so mad, and so frustrated that all I managed was "You must be a complete fucking moron if you believe her" before I walked off.

Needless to say, her behaviour kept getting worse, they kept witnessing it, but kept denying it. Obviously, they didn't want to face up to the fact that their daughter was a nasty, violent savage. They kept denying it and enabling her until the day we split, and even after that they would tell people about how she had to get divorced from me because of how I was, not because she was the problem.

The Unpacking

I must confess, that while he was telling me this story, I was feeling very frustrated too, as I know what it's like to have people believe your abuser over you, even when faced with insurmountable evidence. It's one of those things, that people probably think there is no way that this can happen, but it does, and it does often, and that's the power of a narcissist. They can get people to believe nonsense, or to just be too afraid to challenge the nonsense.

Pre-empting and blame shifting are massive tools that narcissists use, and she has used here, to get their Flying Monkeys to side with them. For people close to them like family members, they will use a combination of fear and guilt to get them on their side. No parent wants to believe their child could act like this, and a narcissist knows that and uses it. For other people like friends and acquaintances, it's easy for them to tell stories the way they want them to be heard, where they are the victim, and you are the abuser. It happens throughout the relationship, and obviously happens plenty when the relationship ends.

If you think about it though, if a friend or acquaintance came to you and told you something terrible that their partner did, you would probably believe them, and wouldn't even think for one second that it was some kind of abusive technique. In those cases, you can't blame them, but in the case of close friends or family who choose to ignore the terrible behaviour, they can definitely be held accountable for refusing to help or stop the abuse.

My opinion, thoughts, advice, or tips

In terms of advice I gave him while we were talking, I literally don't think he could have done anything different. He spoke up, confided in people close to them, agreed an action plan, had them hear the incident live on the phone, and it still didn't work for him. The hold that she had on her family was so strong that he couldn't break it. He told me that no matter what she did after that they just excused it somehow, no matter how bad it got. They were in full denial mode.

For people in similar situations, or for people on the lookout to stop these kinds of things happening, I can say that it is worthwhile having an impartial confidant if able. Someone who isn't under the spell of the narcissist. Obviously, that has the pros of them not being in denial, but it has the cons that the narcissist won't listen to them anyway if they address the behaviour.

If you are helping someone who is the one being abused, just remember it's about gathering evidence for when it can all be stopped and to help it stop, it isn't really about trying to fix it, because you can't fix that type of abuse, and you shouldn't want to fix it, you should want to end it.

Chapter 8: Bend the Knee

This story is from a man who was married to his abuser. They had been together for about 5 years, married for 2. The thing that is interesting about this story, is that it is fairly unique in terms of the specifics. Obviously, everyone's stories are unique, but what I mean is with a lot of stories from abuse victims, there are similarities – like massive blow ups, attacks, false arrests etc, but this one is very specific, and while the types of abuse and tools and techniques are not, the actual details are. You'll see what I mean when you read the story.

The Story

I have so many different stories of incidents, abuse, times when she attacked me, and things that were said or done to me, but this one is something that I always think is just so over the top, so pathetic, and so spiteful that it stands out in my head, and I can't forget it.

It happened over the course of a week or so, and culminated in the main incident that shows how she thought she could treat me.

I hurt my knee playing football. I was running on the pitch, and there was a small hole that I didn't see, and I stepped in it and my knee just went one way while the rest of my leg went another, and I felt something go pop. It was sore, but not that bad, it felt like it was maybe sprained or something and just needed some ice and would be back to normal in a day or two. I went home and showered and put an ice pack on it, and already she was pissed off with that, saying I was looking for attention. I even said it wasn't that bad, and I just wanted to make sure that it was fine the next day for work. As the evening went one, it was swelling a bit more and getting really stiff, and I thought it was just a normal thing, and overnight the swelling would come down with rest and medication.

I woke up in the middle of the night in pain. My knee was pounding, and I couldn't move it at all. If I tried to move it, it felt like a sharp pain shooting down my leg. I didn't wake her up, because she would have been annoyed with that, so I got up, and half hopped, half hobbled to the kitchen to get some more medicine and an ice pack. I sat on the couch with my leg up, ice pack on my knee, and took more anti-inflammatories, but it hurt – a lot. I had tweaked my knees before, and this was the most pain I had ever had in one. I just stayed on the couch because I didn't want to move. I couldn't fall asleep because of the pain, so I was tired and sore. At about 6am I sent my boss a message telling her that I couldn't come in

90

to work that day because of it, and I would go and get it checked out.

I thought I'd wait until my wife was awake and see if she could take me to A&E to get it checked out, as I didn't really want to drive myself there. She got up at about 7:30, but clearly wasn't interested in taking me anywhere. She told me how I was milking it; it wasn't bad, I had even said so myself, and that I clearly was just using it as an excuse to get off work and not do anything around the house. She said she wasn't going to waste her day taking me to A&E because she was meeting a friend for breakfast. I was so tired and so sore, and the last thing I wanted was a fight, so I waited for her to get ready and leave, and then I got dressed. Luckily it was my left knee, and my car was automatic, so once I managed to hobble into it, I could drive just using my right leg.

I drove myself to the hospital, parked, and hopped my way into the A&E waiting room. I was still waiting for x-rays when she messaged me wanting to know where I was as she had got back. I told her I was at A&E and just got told I was being pathetic and to make sure I got milk on the way home, and to make sure I was home in time for dinner because it was my turn to cook.

After waiting a bit more, I got called in for x-rays. I had them done and went back to wait. They called me into a cubicle with the doctor and told me that the x-rays had been sent off to the orthopaedic surgeon, but for now they would send me home with strong pain killers that would let me sleep, and his office would call me to set up an appointment for the next day. I went home (stopping at the local shop for milk and at the pharmacy for my tablets) and told her what they said. She literally didn't care, and still was going with the fact that I was milking it. Her only concern was wanting to know what was for dinner that night. It was about 3PM only, so I said I would order take aways and she could choose, but I needed to take my tablets and sleep as I had been awake most of the night. She wasn't happy with me "being lazy" and sleeping in the day, but the thought of take away kept her happy enough to not fight that too much. I took the tablets and lay down, and while waiting for them to kick in got the call from the doctor's office to set up the appointment for the next day. I told her the appointment was for 11AM the next day, but she already had plans for coffee with another friend.

I slept a bit that night with the help of the painkillers, although the pain did seem to be getting worse and worse, so was still waking me up. The next day I drove myself back to the hospital and went to see the surgeon. He did a scan with a handheld device in his offices and examined my knee fully. He said it was bad, and that the ligament was torn, but there was something else as well that he couldn't quite make out that was interfering with the ball joint in my knee, making that massive pain when I moved. He wanted to get me booked in for a surgery as soon as he had a slot and get it operated on. I went and waited in reception while he checked with his admin team about when they could get surgery booked in for. He said it might be a day or two as there a waiting list, but to keep on the pain killers and keep my leg up until then.

He went to this next appointment, and I waited to get my surgery details. It was going to be 2 more days, but I'd be first that day. I don't remember much about the rest of that day or the day after, but what I do remember was that I ran out of painkillers in the afternoon of the day before the surgery, and I was in absolute agony. I asked her to go and get me more from the pharmacy (which was about a 2-minute drive from our house) but she wouldn't. It's weird the things you remember, but I remember lying on the bed in the spare room that night (I couldn't sleep in the main room because I would "keep her up with my huffing and puffing") watching TV, and being in such pain that it was almost like I was hallucinating, and I remember quite clearly that the movie that was on was "The Island" with Ewan McGregor, from about 1AM. I did eventually fall asleep at about 4AM or so, but then had to be up to go to the hospital for the surgery. It was at 9, so I had to be there at 7. I had to get a taxi, because she didn't want to get up that early to take me, and there was no way I could drive – firstly from the pain, but also, I couldn't leave my car in the car park for however long I had to stay in the hospital for.

I got checked in, and taken in a wheelchair to the ward and the room I would be in. It was a shared room, and there was another guy there who was having surgery after me, and his girlfriend was there fussing over him. I remember being pretty jealous of that.

The surgeon came and saw me, along with the anaesthetist, and they said I'd feel so much better right after but would need to be in the hospital for at least another day, probably 2, to have some physio and make sure everything is OK before I could be sent home.

When I woke up from the surgery, it was amazing how instant the relief was. That massive pain was gone completely, probably helped massively by the drugs they had given me, but it just felt so much better. I was surprised when I woke up that she was there now, sitting in the chair next to the bed on her phone. She hadn't brought me anything, like food, snacks, drinks, but had come I suppose. She said she came to make sure it went fine and would be back tomorrow. That was it. She left, and I went back to sleep. I still remember the other guy coming back from surgery, and his girlfriend leaving and coming back 20 minutes later with a massive bag of KFC for him.

Later that day the physio came to run through the exercises with me and test my range of motion, and then they came back the next day for some light walking. My knee was in a big brace, and they gave me crutches to use. Two days after I went in for the surgery I was sent home. Remarkably, she came to fetch me. She did scoff at the crutches, like I was being ridiculous at using them. We got home and I went to bed in the spare room right away. It was already afternoon, and I ended up sleeping a few hours. When I woke up, she wasn't home. She had gone to dinner with her family. I ordered myself a pizza because there was no way I was going to stand in the kitchen cooking. I went back to bed but woke up when I heard her come home. She didn't check on me, she just went to bed as well.

Then the next day it happened. I was still asleep at about 9AM when she came in telling me to get up because things had to be done. It was a Friday, and her friends were visiting on the weekend for a lunch. She wanted the pool cleaned because it had leaves on the surface and needed to be brushed. We had a very big pool, and the last week I hadn't been tending to it because of my knee, so it was a bit cloudy and had debris on the top. We had someone who came in to do the lawn and the garden, but they didn't touch the pool. I always did that myself as it needed chemicals, cleaning, the weirs emptying, and if you didn't do it properly it got really cloudy and would get algae.

I told her there was no way I could do it because it I would have to walk around the pool brushing it, while on crutches, and I would have to get down on the floor to empty the weir and test the water PH, and I couldn't get down because my knee was in a brace. I had surgery a few days ago only, I shouldn't be doing stuff like that.

She went absolutely ape shit. She was screaming at me full on, about how useless I was, and how I was letting her down, and it's my responsibility as the man to do it, and how I was going to embarrass her in front of her friends by leaving the pool dirty. That guilt tripping lasted about 2 minutes, and then she went straight into full on demanding. Telling me how I better get outside right then and clean the "fucking pool" or she would "make sure I had real problems with my knee".

So, I did. I was a good boy and did what I was told to do. I was too scared not too. I got up, put on some old clothes, and went outside to clean the pool. I couldn't use my crutches and the pool brush at the same time, so had to hop around the pool brushing it. Then the same with netting it. The worst part was getting down to empty the weirs and test the water. I couldn't kneel obviously, and with my knee in a brace it was hard to sit, so I had to basically fall onto the ground and lie down to do it. It was excruciating. It took me over an hour to do because I was moving so slowly. I was in such pain afterwards, but she had other "important" tasks for me to do to make sure everything was fine for her friends the next day. They were all things that she could have either done herself, or didn't actually need to be done that day, like brushing the patio, and wiping down the outside table and chairs. All in all she kept me working for about 2 hours, and then the following day when her friends came over she expected me to do loads more. Every time one of her friends said that they would do something because of my knee, she would interject with a comment about how I was just milking it and could do it.

Not to go into too many details, but I actually ended up back in hospital because of not taking it easy after surgery. The hopping around and not using my crutches caused my spine to rub weirdly and swell, and so I got weird pins and needles through my leg and my knee wasn't healing properly. The whole time I was in hospital again that second time, she never even came to see me. Probably better to be honest, because she wouldn't have had anything nice to say anyway.

The Unpacking

Very specific and very horrible. There is so much going on here, from playing down his pain, to making him take himself to hospital, not being there for surgery, and then making him do physical work after his surgery which caused more damage - this is a terrible person.

It covers so many different types of abuse here – physical, verbal, emotional and mental. Also, so many tools and techniques used here. Fear, threats, The Sledgehammer, isolation, withholding, criticism, and gaslighting.

Even though this story and incident are of such a specific nature, you can see the patterns and behaviours of the abuser are the same.

Some people may think "you say physical abuse, but she didn't touch him?" but to me, this definitely qualifies. Her actions and inactions, and her behaviour led to actual physical pain and further injuries for him. His pain was ignored and belittled, and he was caused harm. That is physical abuse.

My opinion, thoughts, advice, or tips

Opinion, thoughts, and advice on this one are slightly tricky as hopefully this specific type of incident won't happen again, but we all know the general principles, behaviours, and the approach of abusers will be the same, so let's focus on those.

So, what can we tell people who may end up in similar situations? I asked the storyteller if he thought anything could have been done differently, if he feels in hindsight that he could have counteracted her horribleness in some way or eased the suffering he had to go through during this whole ordeal, but he wasn't sure. Certainly nothing while it was happening that came to mind for him, but that is often the case. It's so hard when you are in it, which is why I believe it is so vital to educate people upfront about the world of abuse and narcissism.

I wondered if getting someone else involved may have helped him. Getting a family member or friend involved, telling them about his knee, and the whole process, getting them to help with driving or fetching medicine etc. I thought maybe this would give him some relief and help. He said it was a maybe. He felt that she would react badly to that, see it as more "milking" of the situation, and trying to make her look bad.

He wasn't ready yet to come forward to anyone about the abuse, if he had been, then a hospital visit (two in his case) would have been good opportunities. He could have raised it with the doctor, who could have helped get him in touch with a social worker or support person.

I need to say it again, but evidence! He remembers all of this, but you want to make sure it is documented at the time of happening. A big problem (and we are going to touch on this in more detail in one of the upcoming stories) is that the legal system isn't fair, especially when it comes to men who are saying that their partners have abused them. You can say everything that happened, like he has done here, but your narcissistic abuser will come up with loads of stories about what you "did" to them (with no evidence of course), so the more evidence, more documentation, more detail you have, the better.

Chapter 9: And the Oscar goes to

I "like" this story, not because it is nice, it is horrible, but because it was the incident that sparked this man's freedom. It was the final incident of physical abuse he went through in his own home at the hands of his abusive wife, and something he said he needed to in order to get out and make a new life for himself.

This is another big man, well above average, and significantly bigger than his abuser.

The Story

Height: 6 foot 2 inches

Weight: 97kg/214lbs

Another day in paradise. Stuck at home, with a horrible abusive wife who was getting worse with every passing day. This was during Covid, so we had been in lock down, then out, then back into another lockdown, so we were at home together every day, and it was like living in absolute hell. Lockdown was bad for most people, but for people who were in an abusive relationship it was sheer torment. I no longer got the respite of going to work, for being away from her for a few hours at least. Now it was 24/7, and I just didn't have the courage to leave, and the fact that it was during Covid made it so much harder to think about where I could go, how could I escape, were there even any options for me?

Anyway, I didn't know when I got up that day that this was to be the start of some sort of freedom (physically at least) for me. I just had to go through this to get there, which wasn't great, but I'd rather that then still be there or dead (which I have no doubt I would be if I hadn't gotten out – either by her hand or mine).

I don't know what happened before the incident started, I can't remember at all, but I remember what happened when it all started very clearly. I still to this day have nightmares about it.

I was sitting at my desk in the study doing some work. If I turned my head to the right, I would look out of the study door, through the entry hall, and into the kitchen directly. She was standing in the kitchen and was just badmouthing me. Nothing unusual, and something I just tried to completely ignore because what was the point of getting involved in it. It was pointless, she just wanted to start an argument, and I tried to steer clear of them because they always ended up with me being hurt (physically and emotionally). I don't know what made up problem she was going on about this time, but she always found something to tell me off for, like me not making her tea strong enough, or if I used a tea bag for myself, instead of her used tea bag, because she didn't think I needed to use a new one for myself.

Regardless of what it was, she was doing her usual thing of standing there, talking loud enough for me to hear, but not to me, just saying things out loud about how pathetic I was, what a useless person I was, how she should leave and find someone better, all interspersed with every swear word she knew.

Her tirade was getting louder and more heated, and started to moving more towards how she thinks she should just kill me, because that's what I deserved. I made the mistake of looking over at her when she said that, and she saw me look, which just added fuel to her self-burning fire. I got a "What the fuck are you looking at? Do you want me to kill you, piece of shit?" and she ripped open the drawer and grabbed a carving knife. She started waving it in front of her, spitting and screaming, continuing her theme of how I should die. Unfortunately, this wasn't new either. I think one of the biggest problems was that the more she did, the more she was comfortable with doing, and so her behaviour just kept getting worse.

My hand moved towards my phone, which was usually in my pocket, because I thought I might either need to record her if it got worse or call the police if it got really bad. I realised when reaching for it that it was actually upstairs on charge, but she obviously didn't know that, and she seemed to pause slightly. She put the knife down but didn't stop her mouth at all.

I looked back away to start work again as I thought she would just go back to ranting to herself, but she must have gotten herself fired up with the knife, because she was suddenly coming towards the study. I could tell from the way her face was blood red, her nostrils were flaring, and she looked like a charging rhinoceros that she really wanted to get physical. I got up from my chair and moved behind it, not that it did any good. She just went straight to it, trying to punch me in the face. I'm a lot taller than her, so by standing up straight, raising my shoulders up, and keeping my arm up, I could take the hits on my arm rather than the face which was preferable. This was not a small dainty woman, she was broad and strong, so when she hit it hurt a lot, and she wasn't slapping or holding back, she was punching as hard as possible. I did what I always did and backed away while keeping my guard up. I backed out of the study, back through the entry hall, through the kitchen door, out the other door that led to the dining room, through the dining room, through the lounge, back through the entry hall, past the study again and down the hallway to a crafts room she had, and finally got into the TV room, which was the last room downstairs, and I now had no more doors to back out of. I had nowhere else to go, and she was blocking the doorway. Up until this point, this had been going on for about 5-10 minutes I would guess, and she had punched me so many times. My arms were absolutely killing me, and she had caught the top of my head a few times.

I just covered up, taking hit after hit. She never once stopped the stream of abuse coming out of her mouth either. Telling me how pathetic I was and how I deserved this. I was in serious pain now, with my arms feeling like they couldn't take much more. Enough was enough. I grabbed her and pushed her back into the wall, holding her against it, screaming at her that it was enough. She was furious, and I remember a "you better fucking let me go, I'm going to kill you."

I didn't let go, I held her there up against the wall and I said "I'm done, I've had enough. I'm calling the police." With that I let go and walked straight out of the room, and I was going to get my phone and call the police, tell them what had happened, and what she had been doing to me for years. I had gotten to the top of the stairs when I heard her. I'll never forget her voice, and what she said. It was so fake, so manipulative, so evil, that it literally still haunts me to this day. I heard the whimpering cries, muffled by tears (she could literally cry on demand whenever she wanted, to really put on a good show) of "Help police. My husband has gone crazy. He's attacked me. I don't know what to do. He has mental health issues, please help." For the record I do have depression and anxiety (not surprising now that I think about it) but I was on medication and had counselling regularly, and it was really well managed. It was obviously just a good little weapon for her to use there.

I didn't call the police because she had, and I just went and sat in the lounge and waited for them to come.

They came pretty quickly, I must say. Less than 10 minutes, I think. I heard them pull up, and they knocked on the door, and I answered it. I don't think they expected me to answer because she was the one who called. There were two police officers, a man, and a woman.

I told them to come in, and they did, and they asked where she was. I told them she was in the kitchen, and the lady officer went off to talk to her. I went in the lounge with the male officer, and he asked me what had happened. I told him the story just as I told you now, showing him my arms, and the marks on my head, telling him how it happened all the time, and I had had enough now, and how I wanted to call the police and she beat me to it with her fake call.

We spoke for about 20 minutes, and then he went to talk to his partner, and then he came back, and we spoke for another 10 or so minutes, just going over details so he could write them all down correctly. It was at this point that his partner came in, and she asked me to stand up. I did, and got quite a shock when she said, "You are under arrest for assault", and I didn't even catch the rest of what she said. I was really blindsided by that. I hadn't done anything, and they were arresting me. I had never broken any laws, I paid all my taxes, did everything by the book, and was a good person, but I was being arrested, for being attacked basically. The only interesting thing was that the male officer who had been speaking to me also seemed surprised and asked to talk to her outside. They went off for a few minutes, and then came back and told me that they had to take me to the local station. They walked outside with me and put me in the back of their car, in broad daylight for all the neighbours to see, but they didn't handcuff me, which again I surprised about. If I was being arrested, why wasn't I being handcuffed and all of that? It was about a 25-minute drive to the police station, and I was so nervous. I had never been arrested before, never been in trouble before, and was thinking things like "what about work tomorrow?" I asked them if I could just send one message from my phone to work and they could watch me do it just to let them know I would be off for the rest of the week "due to personal circumstances." They did actually let me do that, and I felt a bit better that I had at least let work know.

They took me in, and I was "processed" and had all of my stuff taken off me like phone, watch etc, and told that I would go to a cell and wait there for a lawyer to talk to me and then be called to be questioned. That was about 2PM I think. I went into the cell and just lay on the bed. My head was spinning in a million different directions, worried about the trouble I could be in because of her false accusations, wondering why they hadn't arrested her when they could see that I was bruised one, but on the other hand I also felt quite safe, because I was in there, and she couldn't get anywhere near me. It was a weird feeling of having two very different emotions at the same time, fear and safety.

I lay on the bed thinking for ages, and eventually the little panel opened, and they said that the appointed lawyer was on the phone. They gave me the phone, and the lawyer asked them to tell me everything, so I did. I told her about that day but also about the abuse prior to that. She told me not to worry, because it will be easy to show it wasn't me, and she will be on the line when they interview me. All I had to do was just tell the truth about had happened and what had happened before. I asked her the time and it was about 7PM.

I lay back down and waited again. Much later, I heard the door being opened, and one of the officers on duty said that the interview was going to happen now. I had to follow them to the interview room, and they said my lawyer would be on the phone there too. I asked them what time it was, and it was just before 11PM.

In the interview room was another officer, and a huge kind of recording device on the table. It looked archaic, like something from a 1970's police show. I could tell from the start that the interviewing officer didn't like me and had decided that I was clearly some kind of wife beater. He was rude, abrupt, and condescending. My lawyer kept interrupting him and telling him to stick to interviewing me about the events of the day, as he kept trying to go off track onto other things. I remember distinctly her asking him how come they were keeping me and doing all of this with me when I was the one covered in bruises, and when they had seen my wife at the house, she didn't have a mark on her, but I was the one taken in. He said it was "protocol" which I think now is just their way of saying that they don't understand men can be abused. We covered the events of the day, and then I got another surprise. They said that my wife had made other claims against me besides assault.

She had told them that I had been drugging her for months and that according to the law, they said that was classed as poisoning. I said that it's a lie, and my lawyer asked if they had any evidence of any of the things that she was saying about me, and he did admit that they did not but "investigations are still ongoing" was his go to line. The interview went on for what seemed like forever, and even at the end the officer conducting it seemed to realise that I wasn't the bad one, as he even said that given that I was bruised all over, and she had no marks, I would most likely be released with no charges, but they did have to investigate further the next day.

I was taken back to my holding cell, but I was only there for a few minutes, and they came to fetch me again to say I was being released. I was taken back to the main area, given my stuff back, and told I would be released, but could obviously not go home while the investigation was ongoing which should be done later that next day. I asked them where was I meant to go? It was lockdown, and I had no family or anything I could call or stay with. They said if I could find space at a hotel, then they could provide me with a letter saying that I had the "right" to stay there (as it was during a lockdown for Covid, the hotels were meant to be for front line workers only). They gave me my phone back, so I started Googling some local places, and eventually managed to do an online booking for a cheap chain hotel back closer to where I lived, about a 20-minute drive from the station.

They called a local taxi company for me and organised a taxi to take me to the hotel. When they let me out finally it was 2AM. It was freezing cold outside, as it was winter, and I had on the clothes I was wearing inside when arrested, so I had no coat or gloves or anything.

The taxi came and took me to the hotel, and they dropped me in the car park. When I got to the reception it was locked up, with a little intercom on the wall. I buzzed in, and they told me that I couldn't come in, and I could only check in the at 10AM, so to come back as they couldn't let me in. I told them the police sent me, but they didn't care. I was standing outside, at 2:30AM, in winter, without a jacket, and nowhere to go. I walked. I walked for hours and hours just to keep warm. I realised after a while that the big local supermarket would open at 7AM, so I could at least go in and get something to eat and drink. I walked around for hours and made my way there when it opened. I took my time there because it as warm, and I couldn't go anywhere else.

At about 8AM I decided to walk to the hotel to try again and see if I could get in early. The lady at reception took pity on me and gave me a room early thankfully. I had a hot shower and went to sleep. The police woke me up by phoning me at about 1:30PM to say that they were done, and I could go back to the house and get some things if I needed to, but I had to go between 2:30PM an 3:30PM, as they knew she would be out.

I went and got my laptop and a suitcase full of clothes and went back to the hotel. I ended up living in that hotel for 2 months during that lockdown, with no restaurants open, no microwave, no oven, nothing except a kettle. I lived off of cheese and crackers and pot noodles. It was horrible, but much better than being abused daily.

It was a terrible thing to go through, but it was the kick I needed to get away from her. After that, I filed for divorce, and I have moved on with my life.

The Unpacking

This is a truly heartbreaking story (as are all of them), because an innocent man, and a victim, had to go through not only abuse, but also the fear of arrest and punishment because of his abuser, and it is truly heartbreaking because all of that had to happen for him to finally get away from her. It definitely shouldn't have to be that way.

In terms of type of abuse, we have a lot here – physical, emotional, verbal, mental, but let's focus in on the tools and techniques she used.

There was fear, and threats, but I want to spend a bit more time looking at the tools of blame shifting and pre-empting.

She used pre-empting heavily to her advantage by calling the police before he had a chance to, so she pre-empted the events into a story where she was the victim. It just shows that even in moments of rage and panic, a narcissist can still employ their tools easily and effectively, it's in built to them, and second nature.

She has blame shifted everything to him, making him the abuser, and not only did she blame him for what had happened that day, but she added in extra items to try and make the blame even worse.

My opinion, thoughts, advice, or tips

I have a lot to say about this one, as I had similar experiences, being wrongly accused and facing police action against me, despite being the victim and not the abuser.

It is hard enough for male victims of abuse as it is to come forward and be believed or taken seriously, but when you have a narcissist actively trying to lie, blame shift, pre-empt, deceive, manipulate and so on, it becomes even harder. This man was covered in bruises. His abuser had none. But still, he was the one arrested, he was the one who had to go through a scary ordeal after being beaten, and then be interrogated and made to feel like he was going to be punished.

It seems such an easy thing for people to do - whether they are police, court officials, or just friends and family - to just believe that it must be the man who is the abuser. In the UK, recent statistics from the Office for National Statistics (ONS) revealed that an estimated 13.2% of the male population experienced domestic abuse in the last year alone. And bear in mind many men don't come forward because of fear of shame, embarrassment, and being treated like the abuser.

Only once parity is achieved, and officials realise that anyone can be abused, will this start to change.

Not only shouldn't this man have been arrested in the first place, but once they finally acknowledged that it wasn't him, they should have charged his abuser.

I personally was on the receiving end of bad treatment from police, and also from the court system, which is something we will discuss more in the next story.

My one big piece of advice in this kind of situation, and something I said to my storyteller was this: he should have phoned the police anyway. He should have phoned and told them what had happened, so that his call was on record too. Because it wasn't, the only recorded call was hers, so he didn't officially report it. That would have helped him longer term and might have helped him be treated more fairly from the off.

Chapter 10: The greatest works of fiction ever told

We've come to the final story, and I left this one for last, as it deals with abuse after the storyteller was "free" from his abuser. He had divorced her years previously but was still in legal proceedings against her for financial orders, child visitation orders, and a non-molestation order, which is actually the basis of this story. I left it to last as it's important to re-emphasize that getting physically away from your abuser doesn't necessarily stop the abuse, because even though the physical abuse stopped, she kept going with every other kind she could.

The Story

Height: 6 foot 3 inches

Weight: 120kg/265lbs

This is about a particular court appearance I had, as part of the process of making sure the non-molestation order that I had been granted against my ex stayed in place. Before this hearing, I had been to court so many times following the split from her – for financial hearings because she wanted everything, to child visitation hearings to try and be able to formally have something in place around seeing my children, to then non-molestation proceedings to stop her abuse on the phone and messages.

At the financial hearings I was treated like rubbish. They took one look at me (a big, bearded guy) and obviously decided I must be the villain in the story. To be fair to them, they only would have thought that because all of her submissions to the court were claiming she had been a victim of domestic abuse, and how traumatised she was, even claiming she had PTSD. My submissions were all focused on what the hearing was about at the time, like financials or child arrangements etc, but she always included things that had nothing to do with them, and all to make me look like a terrible person. She had crafted her whole narrative around the fact that she was a poor victim, standing up to the mean abuser, and she would cry and sob in every hearing, and ask for breaks because it was too much for her. Because I wasn't doing any of that, I must have just looked like some remorseless scumbag.

Anyway, I was used to seeing her documents for court containing lies and this narrative, and obviously they never came with any evidence, as she didn't have any.

Sometime into all of these proceedings, I was getting really fed up with messages she would send me whenever I tried to message to arrange to see the children. She was always rude, condescending, or would make ridiculous requests. She would often call screaming at me telling me I was late when pickup or drop-off was still 30 minutes away. I was undergoing counselling for everything that had previously happened anyway, and I raised this with my therapist who said I had to set boundaries and use a third party and not have anything more to do with her as it was really bad for my mental health, as I was still being abused.

I decided that it was time to put a stop to it, so I applied for a non-molestation order, without notice. All that means is that the first hearing will be just me, and she won't be told about it, so that I can plead my case to the court, and then they will decide if it gets granted or not. Even if it does get granted, you still must then have another hearing where the other person can come to defend themselves. If it gets upheld or they don't show up, it is in place for a year or 6 months, depending on what was awarded. Well, that's how it works in England at least where I am.

I got an email saying that an appointment had been set for a without notice hearing and it would be in 2 days' time. I was really happy with that, that they hadaccepted it to be without notice, and it would happen soon! I had to prepare a brief pack, with evidence, to show why I thought it should be granted, and why I thought it was urgent and should be done without notice. I got everything ready to go, with pictures, text exchanges, and other evidence of her behaviour both past and present.

I wasn't sure what to expect when I was called in at the court, I just assumed it was one judge, but it was actually 3 magistrates. They were all ladies, and then there was one legal advisor.

They did start off by telling me that a without notice hearing was very rare to grant, and that it was even rarer still for a non-molestation order to be granted without notice. That made me nervous, because I really didn't want to be in court doing the hearing with my ex there.

I made my case, provided them with the evidence pack, and they went off to deliberate. They came back and said the order was granted! It was such a massive relief for me. Not just that it was granted, but that I wasn't treated like rubbish or the abuser and was actually being listened to. They explained that I would have to come back for the second hearing where she could defend herself, but it was in place for now and she would be served with it. They said they would make a note that on the day of the second hearing, I could have a sperate waiting room, and there would be big dividing screens put up in the court so I wouldn't have to see her. That was something!

I got an email a week or so later with the date of the next hearing, and what I had to prepare and submit for it in advance. It was basically a pack similar to the last one, saying why it should be upheld for the year period, and providing evidence. I got it all ready and submitted it via email to the court. I heard nothing more about it before the day of the hearing.

I got to court that day early, just to make sure that I was there and could take the time to breathe and calm down before it started. I find court really nerve wracking, the second I enter I get nervous, so getting there a bit early helps.

I got there, signed in past security, and was shown to my sperate waiting room. They told me that she was already there in another waiting room, which wasn't great – I was really hoping she just wouldn't show, but of course someone like her was never going to "admit" to any wrongdoing by not fighting tooth and nail against any accusations.

I knew it would be a long wait, I was about 40 minutes early, and they always run late anyway, but I didn't think it would be an eventful wait. Turned out it was.

A few minutes into my wait, one of the court staff came to me and said that I had not received a copy of my ex-wife's bundle, so they were going to print it out for me to read before the hearing started. Not great, because I should have got it days before to be able to go through it properly and prepare, and instead I was getting it right before.

They came and gave me the pack once it was printed, and I read through it. It was massive, like all her submissions. Mine was about 8 pages (including evidence pictures) and hers was over 30 pages, all text.

I read this monstrosity and couldn't believe my eyes (well I could given what kind of person she is, but even for her this was bad), and I'll say that is the greatest work of fiction I have ever read. It would put Stephen King, JK Rowling, and any other bestselling fiction authors to shame in terms of the imagination that went into this.

The entire submission was made up stories of abuse that she had "suffered" at my hands, of my terrible mental health and how she was scared and blah blah blah blah. The most absolutely absurd thing about it was that they were so over the top, and so ridiculous, that only a complete idiot could believe them, but yet her solicitor had still submitted them, and the court had received them. To me, I just thought that she would get in massive trouble for lying in official court documents.

Now, I bet a lot of people say that whatever their ex has said is ridiculous, but this really was out of this word stuff, and I'll give you two examples of what I mean.

Firstly, she claimed loads of physical abuse at my hands (and there was none at all, plenty from her on me though), but she even went into a detailed story about how one day I had grabbed her round the throat one handed, lifted her off the floor, held her in the air, and then thrown her from the kitchen so that she landed in the lounge on a small coffee table, hurting herself badly. You might think when I say that "Well you are a big man, might be true", until you know the facts. Sound rude to say, but this woman is fat. Really fat. She weighs about the same as I do, even though she is nearly a foot shorter. I wish I was that strong, to be able to lift someone with one hand that weighs about 120kg, and hold them up, and throw them. Maybe if I was Darth Vader. Now the second fact to know, is the distance she claims that I did this miracle one handed feat of strength over is about 4 metres/13 foot. And before you think well maybe it happened and she is just exaggerating, and you pushed her, I didn't. It never happened at all. I thought this was a clear example of how they would read this drivel and realise she is making up stuff as she goes along.

Second example is probably my "favourite" out of all the lies she put in this fiction fest. She claimed that not only had I been trying to kill her for ages, by poisoning her drinks, but she claimed that the police had interviewed me about it, and I had confessed to doing it, and they didn't do anything about it, and told me to not do that anymore. She really wanted people to believe that I confessed to attempted murder, and the police were like "naughty boy, don't do that anymore please". I saw this lie as the slam dunk that would prove to the judge how dangerous she could be with her lies.

When they called me in to court to take my seat (on my side of the dividing screens) I felt pretty confident. Something I forgot though was that I was a guy, and a big guy, and I looked the way I looked, and I couldn't turn on the water works whenever I felt like it. It was by far the worst hearing I have ever been in, and I was treated like I was guilty from the off.

The judge was a man about 55 years old I'd say. He had obviously had a scan through our submissions prior to coming out, and it was very clear that he had decided she was the victim, and I was the abuser, even though it was a hearing for my petition, and they had already granted the non-molestation in my favour without notice.

She was "crying" and he spoke to her like she was a dainty flower that might wilt in the court room lights, offering her time, asking the helper to bring water for her, and telling her to take her time. When he addressed me, he might as well have just spat at me. He was rude, aggressive, demanded I stand up when he spoke to me, and made his feelings clear from the off. He wouldn't let me elaborate on any answers to questions he asked me, and if I tried to, he would interrupt me and tell me to stop. He even said that with all her allegations, maybe he could look at granting her a non-molestation order against me. Again, let me reiterate, she put stories, with no evidence, no pictures, no messages, nothing. I had pictures, text exchanges, formal reports.

Luckily for me, he was either lazy, or pressed for time, because he said he wasn't going to dive into everything that day, so he would set a new hearing to go through all the evidence (even though it was just mine and not hers), but because the court was so backlogged, it would only be in about 4-6 months' time. He kept saying after that how he hoped I would just drop it to "not waste the court's time". And that was it, a hearing where I just got treated like shit and then nothing was actually done. The only positive being that the non-molestation order was still in place.

I was really angry at that judge, the way he spoke to me, the way he acted, the fact that he literally could buy into such obvious lies, and the way he clearly had it stuck in his mind that the man must be the abuser, despite all of the evidence to the contrary. I filed a formal complaint with the court about him on their online complaints system, but it was just ignored.

It left me with a real fear of the legal system because it showed that it wasn't about evidence or truth, it was about whatever you felt like saying, and no one can say more or make up more than a narcissist, so where did that leave me?

One of the worst parts of it was that in subsequent hearings for other matters, she used that judge as "evidence" in her submissions, saying that the judge on that day realised that she was the victim because of "all of the evidence she had submitted". She didn't have any evidence! So, a lie on top of a lie!

I didn't even get any paperwork from the court after that hearing, to say what had happened. Months later, I went into the local police station just to get them to check and make sure that the non-molestation order was actually in place, and they confirmed it was.

The Unpacking

I'd love to say I was surprised by this story, but I wasn't. This pretty much mirrors my own court experiences, as well as the lies my abuser came with. And, unfortunately, the court treatment has been something that many men I have spoken to have shared.

In terms of tools used here, we have a variety – fear, gaslighting, pre-empting, blame shifting, and criticism. It's so important to remember that a narcissist will never take the blame, so they will use whatever tools they can to try and avoid it, and they want you to look like the one who is the abuser, not them.

The huge problem in this story, and often in the world in general, is that these tools work. She made up ridiculous lies about him, but instead of getting punished for lying in a formal court submission, she got the judge on her side with them. It is really disheartening, but with more awareness and more people speaking up, it will change.

My opinion, thoughts, advice, or tips

Having heard this same type of story many times from men I have spoken to, and from having experienced the exact same thing myself, I feel that I am in a decent position to give some good advice on this.

My first piece of advice, is do not represent yourself in court against a narcissist. Easy to say, but finances can make that impossible, as lawyers, solicitors, and barristers are expensive. It should be simple enough to represent yourself in basic hearings like these, but when you have to try and counter lies and manipulations, it's better to have someone there with you. Firstly, they will know the actuals laws that have to be addressed, whereas you will want to argue on what's right and fair, but secondly, the judge will deal with them, not you, so you can't be treated badly directly.

Some more advice if you do get a lawyer/solicitor etc, is to only communicate the necessary things with them, don't go into emotional areas, because that's costing you money. You have lost enough to your abuser; you don't want to throw more money away after them as well.

Other tips for court I can give is to dress nicely. Look smart, look presentable, be polite. It makes a difference to how the court perceives you. If you walk in wearing a t-shirt and shorts and your abuser is dressed nicely and putting on the fake tears, you just look like you don't care. I hate that, because I don't believe in being anything except who and what you are, but it can help a little so why not do it.

Last tip – for any documentation or submissions you have to prepare, be concise and be factual. Make it easy for the court to see your points, understand where you stand, understand what you are asking for. In my appearances where I have done that, they appreciate it.

My final thoughts on this are that it is really sad. When men get treated this way by someone in power, it is because the myth is still prevalent that men must be the abusers. I am 100% against abuse of any kind on anyone, male or female, and I hope that no victim ever gets treated badly, but people do need to be more educated around the fact that abuse can happen to anyone. I hope that everyone in the world who is trying to raise awareness for abuse, realises that they should raise awareness for all abuse. Obviously, you have a niche you may support or campaign for, like I am writing a book here about male abuse victims, but it doesn't mean you should ever try and take away from anyone else. I have seen too many campaigners try and "outdo" the opposite gender abuse campaigners, like saying things like "oh women get abused more than men so worry more about women" or vice versa, but we should never try and stop awareness, we should add to it.

Final Thoughts

So, there we have it, ten stories of different incidents of abuse from men who have suffered at the hands of their partners.

We've seen incidents of all different types, we've seen multiple forms of abuse, and we have seen the many tools and techniques that abusers use against their victims on show in these stories.

These stories are really important for a few reasons.

Firstly, people need to know what happens behind closed doors in abusive relationships. They need to know the different ways that someone can be abused, and that it can happen to anyone, regardless of gender, and regardless of size.

The second really important thing for me is that people read these stories and know that the men telling them in these cases have all made it out of their abusive relationships and are moving on with life. Some at different speeds and in different ways, but they are out of them. It can be done. If you read these stories and think that they sound familiar to you, and you feel that you have no hope of ever getting out, you do.

The last thing to the importance of these stories, is around education. Education on these topics is vital to not only victims and supporters of victims, but to others to make sure that they do not become victims themselves, or if they do, to minimise the pain and suffering they have to endure. It's one thing to learn the theory around the types of abuse and tools and techniques that abuses use (and you must learn about those), but it's another to "see" it in action in a story of what actually happens. Knowledge and understanding are what will start to make the difference around this truly horrible topic of abuse.

For everyone who told their story here, and for everyone everyday who tells their stories and shares knowledge and experience with others – thank you. It is hard to open up, and it is hard to share, but it is so important as well.

No one should be abused. No man, no woman, no child - nobody.

If you know someone who is being abused, or you think they might be, learn more, and help if you can, support if you can.

If you are being abused – it can get better, and you can get out, and you can have a life without abuse. Stay strong, learn, read, reach out, and when the time comes, be ready to leave.

Finally, I would like to add that this book was focused on male victims of domestic abuse, as that is where my experience lies, and it's a topic that is not discussed as openly or as much as domestic abuse against women. This doesn't mean that it is more or less important, just that I am focusing on it here. Abuse needs to end. All abuse. I would encourage anyone who speaks out against abuse to speak out against all abuse, and support others who speak out to.

Please could you take the time to leave a review on Amazon, as this helps other people who need a resource like this to find the book by making it more visible. My goal is to create awareness for these serious issues, and you review helps to do that.

Thank you so much.

Please see the following pages for details around another book on the topics of abuse and narcissism.

WHY DIDN'T YOU JUST LEAVE THEM?

And other ignorant things people say about abusive relationships

JARED WHITAKER

Why didn't you just leave them? And other ignorant things people say about abusive relationships.

"Why didn't you just leave them? Can't have been that bad if you stayed? You're both as bad as each other. Why didn't you tell anyone? Why didn't you go to the police? Was it actually that bad? Is that really abuse? You must like it. Aren't you overreacting? I'd never put up with that. That would never happen to me."

These questions and statements are just a glimpse into the ignorance and damage surrounding discussions on abusive relationships and narcissists. "Why didn't you just leave them?" delves into the depths of abuse, control, coercion, narcissism, and manipulation, shedding light on the misconceptions that plague this often-misunderstood topic.

Written from personal experience of an abused man, this book aims to offer solace and understanding to those who have endured abusive relationships. It serves as a resource for anyone seeking insight into abuse dynamics and how to support those affected. It is a call to share this knowledge with loved ones who may be struggling.

This book challenges stereotypes, highlighting that anyone can be a victim of abuse, regardless of gender, appearance, or background. Through discussions on different forms of abuse and methods of control, the author provides practical advice for survival, seeking help, and healing.

Join the author on a journey of empowerment and education, with practical exercises to aid in understanding and taking action. For those who have questioned, judged, or simply not understood, " Why didn't you just leave them " invites readers to explore the truth behind the mask of abuse and narcissism.

Amazon.com QR Code

Amazon.co.uk QR Code

Scan to find this book on Amazon.

Printed in Great Britain
by Amazon